MW01617148

Published by

Life Raft Media Ltd

www.liferaftmedia.com

© Life Raft Media Ltd 2023

Print ISBN - 978-1-913514-34-1

ISBN (other) - 978-1-913514-36-5

ePub ISBN - 978-1-913514-35-8

Acknowledgements

I would like to thank YOU – my customers, subscribers, website visitors and YouTube viewers – for all your positive feedback and support over the years. Your heartfelt comments and messages have ensured the work at Needs Focused Teaching keeps developing and growing.

Thank you everyone!

Contents

Free training from Needs Focused Teaching:

How to have your students respect you, listen to you and follow your instructions

(free online masterclass).

Classroom Management Success in 7 Days or Less

(free book)

Get yours now at:

www.needsfocusedteaching.com

Foreword by Rob Plevin

The importance of energy, emotions and feelings in terms of behaviour and learning is well known and it's something teachers can have an impact on relatively easily. By addressing the mood in the classroom and attending to the emotional and psychological needs of our students, we can enjoy a reduction in the stress, frustration and disharmony which so often result in unwanted behaviours. In the process, we reduce many of the barriers to learning for our students; free of unpleasant or unhelpful states, they naturally become more attentive and responsive.

To this end my intention was to create a collection of activities to develop connection, focus, creativity and calm in the classroom. I call such activities 'mood changers' – activities that instantly appeal to kids and impact them on an emotional level. The problem I faced was time – or more precisely, a distinct lack of it. For a variety of reasons, the project kept slipping further and further down my 'one day' list until I had to accept I would most probably never get round to doing it. I was about to take out my red pen and cross it off the list altogether – along with my 'fix the bathroom radiator' and 'learn to speak Spanish' projects – when inspiration struck me.

A few years back, a delightfully entertaining book for teachers called 'Invisible Teaching' was doing the rounds in staffrooms round the world. It was written by two very experienced and talented trainers called Dave Keeling and David Hodgson. 'Invisible Teaching' was supercharged with enthusiasm and filled with the kind of activities kids find absolutely captivating. It provided teachers with ready-made, proven ways to raise energy, openness and focus in the classroom, and to rekindle a sense of joy in teaching.

I read it and loved it. And in the spirit of the man who famously loved an electric shaver so much that he bought the company, I bought the rights to the book. It has now become this book.

I've changed a few things to bring it more in line with the Needs Focused Teaching philosophy, swapped out some of the activities, given it a new cover and… voila! You now have in your hands a collection of proven, fun activities to change the mood and energy levels in your classroom, so that applying the principles presented in 'Take Control of the Noisy Class' will be child's play. To be honest, it's really Dave and David you should be thanking for most of the activities, but you can thank me for giving them new life.

Welcome to Change the Mood of the Noisy Class.

Needs Focused Teaching: Good Teachers Making Students Feel Good

How often have you seen a genuinely happy, relaxed student causing mayhem in your lesson? Not often. If you want to see kids following the rules and 'getting stuck in', a great way to start is by simply getting them in a good mood. And we know when students are in that mood. We see proof in the way they participate in discussions, what sort of questions they ask, how they seek help, how they express curiosity, how they treat each other. It's even evident in the way they walk into class.

I have spent time in many schools over the years. I've witnessed some incredible teachers and I've always been fascinated by the magic they create. What is it these brilliant teachers do? How do some teachers manage to get the very best from the most challenging, hard to reach kids in school?

I believe the answer is this simple: they make kids feel good. They make them laugh. They make them feel empowered. They make them feel capable. They make them feel understood, wanted, and valued. Perhaps most important of all, they make them feel good about themselves.

In Needs Focused Teaching, we aim to create an environment which supports key psychological needs of students… in order to make them feel good. The following are just 4 of the benefits of this approach:

1. Increased engagement: when students feel empowered through the provision of appropriate and stimulating tasks, and when their efforts are acknowledged, they are more likely to engage and participate in the learning process.

2. Improved relationships: when teachers make a priority of building positive class community and showing students they understand and care about them, students feel connected and are more likely to feel respected and valued, leading to improved relationships and increased trust.

3. Improved behaviour: by communicating clear boundaries and pathways towards good behaviour, by encouraging students to make appropriate choices and by acknowledging their efforts, teachers can foster a sense of responsibility and accountability – resulting in a significant reduction in behaviour issues and a marked increase in manageability and responsiveness.

4. Positive mental health: when students feel valued, content, connected and empowered, they are more likely to have a positive outlook on life and to feel confident in their abilities.

I first came across the idea of a needs-based framework as a model for behaviour in William Glasser's 'Choice Theory' and David McClelland's 'Acquired Needs Theory'. They both propose that we choose our behaviour in an attempt to meet one or more of the psychological needs that are hardwired into our genetic structure. It's a solid theory which makes more sense to me than any other psychological model and I've been sharing and developing my own version, Needs Focused Teaching, for the last 15 years.

In Needs Focused Teaching we identify just three broad groups of key needs (to keep things simple) as the main motivators for behaviour. Teachers employ a range of strategies to ensure these three key needs are being met in the classroom, and in doing so tend to see a marked reduction in behaviour issues, an increase in engagement, an improvement in the quality of relationships, and the overall level of respect students have for their teacher.

The three key needs are as follows:

1. The need for empowerment (acknowledgement, recognition, achievement, choice, freedom).

2. The need for belonging (connection, relationship, feeling loved and accepted).

3. The need for fun (stimulation, excitement, variety, humour, engagement).

You can learn more about Needs Focused Teaching at my website: www.needsfocusedteaching.com

Great teaching and learning are not just about imparting information, but about connecting with students on an emotional level. A teacher who is able to create a supportive, empowering and rewarding classroom environment can have a profound impact on the academic success and well-being of their students. My hope and intention is that some of the activities which follow will go at least a little way to helping you create such an environment.

Key to Activities

Each activity relates to a particular state – increasing energy, creative thinking, focus, connection or calm – with the intention of creating a student-centred learning environment which increases emotional engagement. The activity description will include one of the following icons, making it easier for you to find the activity most suitable.

Energy

This icon denotes energy. Look for it to bring energy and activity into the classroom.

High energy activities generate movement, action, laughter, fun, excitement and interest. They are used to start a session, a new topic or idea, or to invigorate a flagging group.

Undirected energisers bring the wildness and chaos of the playground into the classroom. This energy can be difficult to control, and some teachers avoid bringing it in; dull and monotonous lessons can be the result. When high energy activities are used effectively they can change the mood in a room very quickly – helping to instill a sense of excitement, engagement and focus.

Calm

This icon denotes calm. Look for it to lower the energy in your classroom by inviting students to settle down and quieten the busyness of their minds a little.

The opposite of the above, calming activities are the equivalent of a group of warriors sitting around a campfire listening to stories from the shaman as they drift into an altered state. Brain scans show that the pattern of alpha waves generated when we are in a calm, relaxed state (as opposed to normal waking state beta waves) enhances learning, retention and recall. Setting up a campfire in your classroom is probably not on the syllabus, but luckily I have some great alternatives for you.

Creative Thinking

This icon denotes creative thinking. Look for it to bring bright ideas into the classroom.

The ability to think creatively is becoming increasingly important in today's rapidly changing world. Encouraging students to think creatively in the classroom can help them develop skills that are essential for success in both their personal and professional lives.

Creative thinking helps students become more innovative and find new solutions to problems. It allows them to approach tasks with a different perspective, thereby helping to boost their confidence and self-esteem. By allowing students to freely express their own (perhaps rather abstract) thoughts and ideas, they feel valued and have more courage to participate fully during discussions and other activities. This has the knock-on effect of raising their motivation, which in turn can lead to increased engagement and better academic performance.

Connection

This icon denotes connection. Look for it to develop connection and a sense of inclusion in your classroom.

One of the key benefits of building connection in the classroom is that it fosters a sense of community. When students feel that they are in a safe and supportive environment and part of an inclusive community, they are less likely to feel overwhelmed and isolated, more likely to participate in class discussions, contribute to group projects, and feel comfortable asking for help.

Connection also leads to improved social skills, such as teamwork and communication, and helps develop a culture of respect and understanding. Students who feel valued and respected are more likely to treat their peers and teachers with kindness and respect.

Focus

This item denotes focus. Look for it to develop positive focus in your classroom.

Focus helps students to concentrate on their work and avoid distractions. It promotes the learning and retention of information, leading to improved test scores and overall academic performance.

Developing focus in the classroom also helps students stay on task and complete undertakings more efficiently, which is a valuable skill in both academic and professional settings.

But perhaps the greatest benefit of learning to focus is that it promotes the development of 'growth' mindset. When students are able to immerse themselves in a task and concentrate fully on their work, they can embrace challenges and put in the effort to learn. Many studies have revealed that growth mindset has positive effects on student behaviour, motivation and academic performance.

Activities to change the mood in your classroom

1

Draw

Time: *5 mins*

Additional Resources: *none*

Students attempt to beat the teacher in an energetic quick-draw competition

A fast and quick energiser that gets the whole group buzzing and focused for the beginning of a session.

The teacher invites the class to stand and make their hands into pretend guns which they must then place by their sides, as if they were holstered. The teacher will then ask them to draw their guns accompanied with a very vocal 'bang'.

The object of the game is for the class to draw quicker than the teacher.

Great fun can be had by building the tension between each standoff. For extra pleasure you may wish to experiment with a varying array of Clint Eastwood sneers and cowboy hats.

2

Paper Tails

Time: *5 mins*

Additional Resources: *1 newspaper*

Students learn strategy in a speedy game of cat and mouse

Clear a space and tear the newspaper into as many strips as there are students. Each student must then tuck the strip of paper into the top of their trousers/skirt, as if they have a tail.

The object of the game is to try and remove as many of your classmates' tails as possible whilst keeping your own tail intact. Once your tail has been removed (it hurts just writing that) you are out. The winner is the person left at the end with their tail in place.

This game requires students to employ physical dexterity, energy, risk and strategy as they must quickly decide when to attack and when to defend. It is also huge fun and a great way to use up your Sunday supplements.

3 You're Fired, You're Hired

Time: *10 mins*

Additional Resources: *none*

Students justify their place within education and learn to focus on how important it is to make a positive contribution

Announce to the group that to be educated is no longer a right in this country, and that the school is now a business and the students its workforce. Then pose this question: 'The school has decided to fire all of the students. Based on your current attitudes and behaviour come up with the three reasons the school gave for your dismissal and then counterbalance this argument by coming up with three reasons why the school should rehire you. What have you contributed to the school environment as a student and what makes you an invaluable member of your school?'

This is harder than it sounds. Over the last six months we have asked this question to hundreds of students and can count the genuine responses on both hands. A student recently responded to the question by shouting out that the school should keep him because he was 'brilliant'. Unfortunately, he could provide no evidence within the school to back that up. On the other hand, a female student answered this question by explaining that she supports her fellow students when she can, gets involved with lots of extra-curricular activities and contributes as much as she can.

Most students do not recognise how lucky they are to have been handed their education on a plate (and in a lot of cases a new building). This activity challenges the students' attitudes towards learning and their school and how it may be perceived by others. It also encourages them to look at the skills and abilities they do have and how they may bring these to the fore.

The point is that if they cannot justify their position in an environment that has to keep them, then how on earth will they be able to justify their position in a working world that doesn't?

4 The Flying Feather

Time: *10–15 mins*

Additional Resources: *2–6 feathers (or balloons)*

A fun, energetic game in which teams keep a feather (or balloon) in the air

Divide the group into teams of six to ten. Each team should stand in a circle. Students must keep the feather in the air by blowing it when it comes near them. The best ones to use are the small duck feathers found in pillows. If the feather touches the floor the person nearest to it throws it back into the air. If the feather touches someone they are out of the round. The winner is the last person to be touched by the feather.

A balloon can be used as a substitute item in this game if there is a shortage of ducks.

5

The Flow Test

Time: *5–10 mins*

Additional Resources: *none*

Students learn about flow and when they achieve it in their own lives by completing a quick quiz

Mihaly Csikszentmihalyi (pronounced me-high cheeks-sent-me- high) offered adults a way of assessing flow – the degree to which we are 'in the zone' during specific activities. Richard Reeves, writer on all things related to happiness, defines flow as the moment when we're so absorbed in a task that we stick out our tongue without knowing it. Children do it whilst colouring in. If it's good enough for adults, it's good enough for teenagers too.

Think of an activity and when you were last feeling flow.

	Yes	No
Did you have a feeling of 'this is the real me'?	☐	☐
Were you excited?	☐	☐
Were you disappointed when you had finished?	☐	☐
Did you think about ways you could do more of the activity or ways you could develop your skill or experience within the activity?	☐	☐
Did you feel energised rather than exhausted?	☐	☐
Did you lose track of real time (time passed more quickly)?	☐	☐

The more yes answers you give to the above questions the higher the flow. People generally do not report high flow whilst watching TV.

We can experience flow in a wide range of activities such as walks, sport, leisure activities, drawing, reading and enjoying good food or company.

6

Superhero

Time: *10 mins*
Additional Resources: *paper and pens*
Students create an alter ego

The reason that education is one of the hardest jobs these days is that we are attempting to educate students for a world in which we have no real idea of what they will actually be doing. What we can do, though, is challenge their thinking and encourage them to explore the idea that nothing is impossible, and that creativity is endless.

The students have five minutes to invent a superhero and name five superpowers that makes them super.

Here is a superhero we prepared earlier:

Name: Super Sally

Superpower 1: Never gets angry

Superpower 2: Excellent driver
(my wife will appreciate this if she ever reads it)

Superpower 3: Can heal people

Superpower 4: Great costume

Superpower 5: Ability to fly

You may like to suggest that the students accompany their list with a picture or at the very least a costume design.

This activity enables the students to be creative, open-minded and above all allows them to entertain the idea of possibility.

7

Have-a-Go Hero

Time: *10–15 mins*

Additional Resources: *paper and pens*

Linking this to the Superhero activity above, the students are required to take a step back from their superhero and one step closer to themselves

Ask the students to imagine they are a superhero in training. They have five assessment levels to pass before they can become a fully-fledged, cape-wearing crime fighter.

They are currently level 1. In groups ask them to come up with activities that could help with their training and begin to develop the sorts of skills that will eventually manifest themselves as the chosen superpowers.

1. 'Never gets angry' becomes 'always pauses before responding, tries to see the other person's point of view and makes time to relax'.
2. 'Excellent driver' becomes 'always indicates at junctions and pays attention to the road rather than talking to passengers'.
3. 'Can heal people' becomes 'trains with St John Ambulance and learns basic first aid'.
4. 'Great costume' becomes 'spends a great deal of time reading fashion magazines and shopping'.
5. 'Ability to fly' becomes 'adrenaline junkie pursuing any of these sporting endeavours: hang gliding, base jumping, paragliding, free running, gliding, bungee jumping, parachuting, cliff diving, wearing jet packs, wing walking, trampolining and that old favourite – becoming a human cannonball.

This activity goes to prove that even superheroes have to start somewhere; that small steps and practice are the keys to developing skills; and that you don't just become great at something overnight – it starts today so that in the future you will be better prepared and able to fight the good fight.

8

Better than 'Hi' or 'Hello'

Time: *5 mins*

Additional Resources: *none*

Students explore one of the most basic human needs – being noticed and acknowledged face to face (without the use of mobile phones)

People like to feel they are noticed, acknowledged and respected. The film Avatar borrows a two-part Zulu greeting: when people first meet, they look each other in the eye and one says, 'I am here to be seen'. The other nods and replies with, 'I see you'. This is a great start to an interaction between people.

The only way to prove this is a superior greeting is to ask students to try it out. The modern 'Hello' or 'Hi' is not so good. According to Stephen Fry on QI the word hello was invented to start telephone conversations because originally there were long pauses following a line connection by an operator.

Agree an appropriate greeting for the class. In the past, teachers would be greeted by a class standing to attention as they entered a classroom and students would sit after the teacher acknowledged the gesture.

Robert Holden, in Success Intelligence, says he uses this as an activity on his courses and asks attendees to greet around ten people using this method. It can be very powerful because being noticed and accepted for who we are is a fundamental part of being human.

9

Say What You See

Time: *5–10 mins preparation time, then a further 5 mins in class*

Additional Resources: *a little research around the school with a mobile phone/ camera or good old-fashioned pen and paper*

Students learn the power of focus by trying to identify common features and landmarks around the school – more difficult and more fun than you might think

Version 1

Walk around the school looking at familiar things with fresh eyes. Make a list of things including their colour, shape and position. Ask students the following types of questions to assess their awareness of their environment:

What colour is the door to the staffroom?

How many chairs are on the stage?

What shape is the reception area?

What is the doormat in the reception area made from and how big is it?

What colour are the curtains in the hall?

How many tables are in the lunch hall, and what shape are they?

Which is taller – the sports hall or the roof of the languages block?

Which is further from the car park – the science block or the English block?

Which chairs are more comfortable – the dining hall or assembly hall?

What kind of tree stands nearest the school gates?

Extend the idea to other things:

Do you know the colour of your toothbrush?

What colour are your pants (without looking)?*

What duvet cover is on your bed today?**

*Unfortunately the colour of many teenagers' pants is no mystery as they wear their trousers so low it is a relief that 'going commando' is not popular these days.

**If it's Fireman Sam or Peppa Pig, and your student is in Year 7 or above, you quietly suggest they pretend to forget.

Version 2

A similar version of this activity is the teacher taking photographs, perhaps on a mobile phone, of close-ups of familiar places around the school and asking the students to identify the location. It is best if the photo can be displayed on a screen for the whole group to see. Alternatively, the teacher could ask the students to take a photo to challenge the rest of the class.

I used to run version 2 of this activity for teams of adults back when I was a corporate trainer. Leaders of well-known companies paid a fortune for their staff members to run around the Lake District trying to locate gate posts, telephone boxes, signposts, rocks and other items from a handful of polaroid photos they'd been given as part of a team-building exercise. It was the simplest activity we offered and easily one of the most popular. Good enough for Mars International… good enough for the classroom!

10

Three and One

Time: *3 mins*

Additional Resources: *none*

Students give you priceless information about their learning preferences

At the beginning of the lesson ask the students in pairs to focus on three things they would like to gain from the lesson (fun, learn something new and cash are the top three you'll encounter on a regular basis). Also ask for one thing they do not want (to be bored is usually the most frequent answer).

Armed with this information the teacher can then craft a lesson that has the buy-in from the students as it is they who have generated the objectives and direction. This is an incredibly useful technique for anyone to quickly ascertain the mood and desire of a group.

This activity gives the power back to students and asks them to take some responsibility for their learning.

11

Fight or Flight

Time: *10 mins*

Additional Resources: *A4 paper*

A competitive game in which students attempt to make the paper aeroplane that will fly furthest. In the process they learn an interesting lesson about the role risk plays in life

Ask the group to each make a paper aeroplane using a sheet of A4. Offer the group a challenge within the following rules of engagement:

- Each person should take their plane and stand touching the wall at the back of the class.

- Each person is only allowed one throw.

- The person whose plane touches the wall opposite without it touching the floor, ceiling or other walls/ windows from the furthest distance is the winner.

- Each person can choose how close to stand to the target wall.

- Ask people to throw in order of height or oldest to youngest.

The safe thing to do is stand close to the target wall to ensure a hit. The high-risk strategy is to throw from a long distance – increasing the chance of winning if you hit the target, but decreasing the chances of hitting the target at all. Usually, boys risk more than girls in this activity.

Life is about balancing risk and safety. The skill is to work out the rules for each of life's challenges. People throwing later have an advantage over those throwing earlier. This replicates the value of experience in life.

12 Wrong Hand, Right Hand

Time: *10 mins*

Additional Resources: *none*

Students learn that habits can be liberating or constraining whilst putting on their socks and shoes with their wrong hands

Ask students to remove their socks and shoes. Working alone they must put on their socks and shoes, but they can only use one hand (their non-preferred hand, i.e. their left hand if they're right handed).

This is difficult! It is a game best enjoyed in the winter months as the smell from some teenage boys' feet in hot weather can be genuinely distressing for anyone in close proximity. And rather than being embarrassed, they are usually prouder than a new mother showing off her baby to an elderly relative.

Ask students to remove their jackets (and ties if you would like to extend the activity). Working this time in pairs, again only using one hand each, they must replace the items.

Habit makes us really skilful. It is only when we have to try something in a totally new way that we realise how valuable habits are. Habits are useful for straightforward tasks in life but can stifle long-term growth. Working in teams and supporting each other produces better results on complex tasks.

13
What's the Use?

Time: *5 mins*

Additional Resources: *none*

Students use their creativity and divergent thinking to come up with a myriad of uses for everyday objects.

A great opener to get students thinking in a different way, this game never fails to produce surprising results.

In pairs or groups, the students must come up with as many creative uses for the object of your choice. You could suggest:

A belt

A box

A paper clip

A bowl

A plaster

When the time is up the students get to feed back their answers. The winner is the group that generates the most creative application. *To give you a flavour, we'll take a belt as our object and give it a whirl now.*

A belt could be used as: a piece of rope, necklace, bracelet, dog collar, shoelace for a big boot, lasso, head band, for making a loud noise, weapon, pretend snake, bag strap, sling, bandage, to hold up baggy socks, as a restraint, to slide down a zip wire, to bite on when your leg is being chopped off, missile, stencil for the letter 'O', to measure the amount of spaghetti required to… you get the picture.

The beauty of this activity is you can't get it wrong; you simply have a go. No ideas are to be pooh-poohed, as every idea is valid and must be made note of; this means ALL your students get involved. It's a great way to break down some of the barriers to learning.

14

'Ave it!

Time: *5 mins*

Additional Resources: *none*

Cockney larfs aplenty in this energy-raising winner

This is a brilliant slant on an old favourite.

The class are required to stand or sit in a circle. To pass the energy in a clockwise motion each person (and in their best cockney accent) must shout "Ave it'. To pass the energy around the other way you must rebuff 'Ave it' by shouting 'Leave it'. To send the energy across the space you must make eye contact and point at someone opposite in the circle and shout 'Oi Roxy', to which that person replies 'Get aht of my pub'. Then the game continues in a clockwise motion with "Ave it' or until someone decides to shout, 'Leave it' or 'Oi Roxy'.

This game brings fun and focus and is a superb way to get students involved as a starter or energizer in any lesson.

15

Flog the Unfloggable

Time: *10 mins*

Additional Resources: *none*

Students are given the opportunity to think on their feet and use their imaginative powers to influence the group

Split the students into pairs. The task is to bring each pair to the front where you will present them with a new product (written on a piece of paper – you won't be required to manufacture a working prototype). They then have sixty seconds to sell this new product to the group. The more ridiculous the product, the more the students will be required to act and think fast.

Give it a go now and try to think of ways you could flog these products:

Cheesy Beer

Leather Socks

Savoury Fruit

Garlic ice cream

Pretend Friend

Rubber House

Edible Car

Encourage the students to think of the product's USP (unique selling point). What are its positives? Could its worst feature be its best? Is there anything like it out there already?

Can they come up with an inventive tagline to promote it? Looking for the positives in any given situation is a tremendous skill and worth developing.

This activity allows students to cut loose and try as hard as they can to make divergent links in a bid to win over an audience – something they will all be required to do many times over when they leave school. Especially if they end up on The Apprentice.

16 Occupational Therapy

Time: 15 mins

Additional Resources: none

Students get to focus on the person they need to be to do the job they want to do

Ask a student to tell you what job they want to do when they are older.

In groups give the students five minutes to discuss exactly what type of person would be brilliant at that particular job. What skills would they have – are they brave, good at solving problems, motivated, compassionate? What would their personality be like – are they outgoing, kind, a bit mad? Where would they live? How would their friends describe them? How much do they earn? What would the day-to-day job consist of? What would they be wearing? How much training would be involved? What is the best/worst part of the job? What would they do in their spare time? Did they go to university, study online, or set up their own business?

Over a very short space of time the class will have built up a profile of the sort of person who might do that job and also what that job might entail. You can then ask the original student if that is the sort of person they aspire to be and, if not, what they would change.

In our experience a lot of young people may say they want to do a particular job because it sounds good or they saw someone on tv doing it. While there is nothing wrong with this, sometimes it pays to really exhaust all the aspects of a profession to work out whether they really like the sound of it or not.

17 The Ultimatum Game

Time: *10 mins*

Additional Resources: *pretend cash notes (optional)*

Students recreate a classic psychological experiment. Will greed or fairness prevail?

Inform students that they are going to recreate a classic experiment. Students should pair up with someone who isn't a close friend. For example, ask people to line up using random factors such as hair colour (darkest to lightest), height, age, alphabetical order (perhaps the third letter of their surname). You could also try this game by pairing friends with each other to see if the results are different.

They are invited to try the following experiment. One person (choose randomly, e.g. tallest or nearest to the door, or toss a coin) is asked to imagine they have been given £100 and can offer to share any amount with their partner from £1 to £99. If the partner agrees to take the amount offered, both keep their share. If the partner refuses, neither gets any money. They only get to make one offer. Insist on no talking whilst the student with the money ponders the offer they are about to make. Give out Monopoly money to add realism (best not to sow the seeds of temptation with real cash). After each pair is finished discuss the results. Who refused? Who accepted? What amounts were offered and why?

In the original study it was discovered that most people offered half or between £40 and £49 to their partner. If the offer was below £20 it was usually rejected meaning neither player received any cash. The experiment contradicts game theory and the standard economics view that people will accept any offer because having something, even a pound, is better than nothing. The experiment shows that people are also interested in fairness and sharing. How do your students compare?

18

Alone or Together?

Time: *10 mins*

Additional Resources: *none*

Are humans more successful when they cooperate or when they compete? In this activity students get an answer

Present the following information and question to your students. Ask students to work in pairs or small groups:

Alan makes an axe head in three hours and a handle in four hours.

Beverley makes an axe head in two hours and a handle in one hour.

Are they better off working together or alone? Why? There are three basic combinations:

1. Working alone Alan would take seven hours and Beverley three hours to make a complete axe.

2. If Alan made two axe heads and Beverley two axe handles and they swapped one each, Alan would work for six hours and Beverley two hours. They would both save an hour compared to working alone.

3. If Alan made two axe handles and Beverley two axe heads and they swapped one each; Alan would work for eight hours and Beverley four hours. They would both work an extra hour each compared to working alone.

Axe head   Axe handle   Axe

If we assume humans vary in their skills and abilities, then cooperation benefits the species. This is a point noted by evolutionary biologists (and hippies in communes). They argue that cooperation has helped humans become such a dominant species. No other species cooperate as much as humans. Axes can be substituted for most objects made by people.

We live in a very social and interdependent world. For example, there is probably no single person in the world that could make a computer mouse by hand – even if they had a decent 3-D printer. It requires someone to drill for oil, collect it, turn it into plastic, mould it into the shape for the mouse, design the technical parts, attach it, transport it and so on.

19

My Round

Time: *5 mins*

Additional Resources: *1 empty 75cl long-neck beer bottle and a £10 note*

The students are set a problem to solve that will test their powers of deduction

This trick is one of my favourites. You simply lay a £10 note flat on a table and place the empty bottle on its head on top of it. You then say to the wide-eyed crowd you have gathered around you, 'This is an incredibly difficult challenge and I bet that no one can whip the tenner out from under the bottle without knocking it over. You can have three attempts: you can touch the tenner but you cannot touch the bottle and whoever is successful can keep the tenner.' This last bit ensures that you never run out of willing participants. It is also a sure-fire way to get everyone in the immediate vicinity pumped full of dopamine (dopamine is a naturally occurring neurochemical that is released in anticipation of or in receipt of a reward). Don't forget though that it is the build-up banter at the beginning of this trick that is the key to its success.

Make a big deal out of this stunt being difficult and play on words like 'whip' and accompany this with a hand gesture; this will suggest that the only way to do this is to use force. Next, you stand back and watch the rusty cogs of invention kick in. It is fascinating to listen to the conversations that will take place regarding angles, speed and force of pulling, not to mention the number of times you will be asked to repeat the rules for task at hand.

Like any good trick the answer is quite straightforward but requires the ability to think a little more laterally. As the saying goes, 'slow and steady wins the race'. To remove the tenner without knocking the bottle over you simply start at one of the short ends end and carefully roll up the note. Gradually, it will push the bottle off leaving the bottle still standing, your £10 safe, a lot of young children with eyes and mouths wide open and a lot of teenagers thinking you're a smartarse. Choose your audience well.

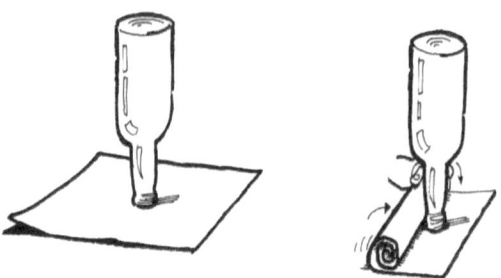

There is a tremendous book called A Hundred Ways to Win a Tenner by Paul Zenon and it is crammed full of clever little tricks like this to confuse, befuddle and more importantly, fleece your friends in the pub.

20

A Helicopter Ride

Time: *10 mins*

Additional Resources: *none*

Students are invited to take an imaginary helicopter ride, meeting friends around the school to demonstrate one of the most important aspects of wisdom

The teacher reads this script to the students. Students need to settle down first and be quiet.

I'm going to invite you to use your imagination to demonstrate one of the most important aspects of wisdom. Imagine a small, toy helicopter resting on top of your head. Feel the weight of it and see its colour. Feel your hair move slightly in the draft of the blade as it spins. Imagine a tiny version of you is going to fly the helicopter. Close your eyes and imagine taking control as you fly your helicopter a little above your head. As you hover above your head take a look at yourself through the eyes of you as the helicopter pilot. Fly your helicopter down near ground level and look up to see yourself. What are your thoughts? What do you like about what you see? What don't you like?

Fly your helicopter into the heads of people you like and people who like you. While in their heads, imagine you can read their thoughts. What do they think of you? What do they like most about you? What do they think you could achieve in your life? Fly your helicopter anywhere you want. Find out what you can learn.

This apparently simple activity replicates a method used by creative thinkers (image streaming is described by Win Wenger and Richard Poe in their book The Einstein Factor), negotiators (Gandhi's was about walking in his opponents' shoes) and anyone able to change their mind about something important such as overcoming a debilitating phobia. In NLP (neurolinguistic programming) it is called dissociation.

21 Doodler

Time: *5 mins*

Additional Resources: *pens and paper*

Students get to chat without talking and learn to work together

Anyone who is looking to form and develop positive relationships knows that the key to this is communication. There are many ways to communicate other than verbally and this activity allows the students to explore openness and to respond and communicate in a more intuitive way.

The class are split into pairs. Each pair has one piece of paper and a felt-tip pen and must decide who is person A and who is person B.

When the time begins, person A must make an intuitive doodle, a line, a pattern or a mark on the paper, then person B must respond to this squiggle with their own doodle. In effect it will become a non-verbal conversation through pictures and shapes.

The key to this working well is not to plan what you are going to draw but to go with it and respond purely to what you see and feel. The results are often very revealing and other members of the class can very quickly work out what sort of conversations/relationships were being formed just by looking at the resulting work.

22 Ten Ten Ten Challenge

Time: *5 mins*

Additional Resources: *none*

Students attempt to solve a puzzle presented to the group to encourage creative thinking

Draw a row of three 10s and ask students: 'Can you convert these three 10s to 950 by adding just one straight line?'

10 10 10

Invite students to have a go. They may need a little bit of encouragement. After two or three volunteers have tried you can reveal the answer.

Answer: Draw a line across the 1 of the middle 10 revealing:

10 TO 10

(i.e. 9.50 – the time, 10 minutes to 10, expressed as a number).

Share the learning points of the activity (assuming that nobody guessed correctly). We are often afraid to volunteer for fear of failure, of making a mistake and looking stupid before our peers and the teacher. If we are not open to try things in life we will never learn, grow and develop. Congratulate any volunteers as they demonstrated bravery in overcoming the fear of failure – a massively important and helpful aid to learning.

Alternatively, if somebody solved the puzzle, congratulate the person on thinking laterally and being open to thinking differently and creatively to solve a problem.

Note: It is best to write up the puzzle rather than speak it. If you speak then say 'nine hundred and fifty' rather than 'nine fifty' as the latter version gives a huge clue to the solution.

23 Why Are We Learning This, Miss?

Time: *5–10 mins*

Additional Resources: *none*

Students are invited to find an answer to a question probably asked in classrooms across the known universe.

Has a student ever asked you, 'Why do we need to learn this subject, Miss?' You may ponder the same question yourself on a hot Friday afternoon as your mind drifts to thoughts of your first mouthful of wine that evening. This activity can provide answers for both you and your student.

Ask the student to step forward and draw themselves in the middle of the whiteboard/flipchart sheet. Ask them to identify skills they use in your classroom and add these around their picture.

Some skills may be general – such as communication, listening, working together, researching, and summarizing. Others may be subject specific – such as percentages, fractions and algebra.

Ask the student or class to nominate a significant life theme, such as happiness, marriage, global warming, holidays, parenting and so on.

Ask students how the skills listed can assist the chosen life theme. Expect some very interesting as well as some frankly bizarre answers. The result is that your subject becomes more relevant to your students – and you're ten minutes closer to that glass of wine.

24

Which Would Win?

Time: *5 mins*

Additional Resources: *none*

Students get to justify their decision-making process in an open and focused thought-provoker

This is a great activity. It's how well students can justify even the most bizarre argument. You can employ this at the start of a lesson or straight after a break as a way of getting minds focused back onto learning.

Ask the students to shout out two random things, for instance Elephant and Banana.

You then write the objects on the board thus:

Elephant

vs

Banana

Challenge the group to chat in pairs and discuss which would win. Be deliberately vague as the students will have to decide what sort of contest it is. For instance, if it was simply a fight, you may think that the elephant has the advantage, but if it were about which one is better to nosh on after a long run then the odds might be in the banana's favour. As long as the students can justify their response, anything goes.

Remember to explain that they cannot get it wrong – they can only contribute. One of the great (and not so great) things about human beings is that there will always be someone to disagree with and so... the debate goes on.

This game lets students' thinking loose, and more importantly encourages verbal reasoning and asks the question, why do you think like you do?

25

Teacher's Pet

Time: *throughout entire lesson*

Additional Resources: *none*

Students get to realise that your talent lies in the choices you make

At the beginning you must nominate who will be the teacher's pet for that lesson. From then on whenever you present a question to the group it must go to the teacher's pet first. At this point the teacher's pet has two options:

Have a guess = 1 point

Nominate another student to have a guess = 0 points

Great fun can be had by either having a guess or stitching up their mates. Either way, across a term it means everyone can have a go at choosing to take responsibility for their learning in a bid to gain the most points and officially become teacher's pet.

The overall winner gets an apple/prize of your own choosing from the teacher and a dead arm from their mates.

This exercise enables the students to look at the power of choice and the fact that it doesn't really matter how smart you appear to be – if you consistently make the wrong choices for your life and learning, the world will never find out how clever you are.

26 Warm Welcome

Time: *2 mins*

Additional Resources: *none*

Students give each other the time of day

There is no better way to set the overall tone of a lesson than at the beginning.

At the start of the session ask the students to give each other a warm welcome. They will do this by shaking the hand of the person sitting next to them at their desk (or everyone on their table), saying 'good morning' or 'good afternoon' and either giving them a compliment or offering one reason why they are looking forward to working with them that lesson. It is a bit like speed dating for beginners but a lot less awkward and expensive.

This is a lovely little warm-up activity that helps lighten the mood and create a relaxed and supportive working environment.

Past, Present, Future

Time: *15 mins*

Additional Resources: *none*

Students discuss their successes and in doing so realise how far they have come

We all have days when we think we haven't really achieved much and wonder why we bother. Sometimes it is worth reminding ourselves on a regular basis how much we have achieved and how far we have come.

This activity requires the students to come up with a success or achievement from over five years earlier, one within the previous two weeks and something they hope to achieve in the future.

Once the students have had time to think through their list of three achievements, the activity can then be opened up to the class for debate. Questions such as the following could be asked. What skills

did you already have to help you achieve this particular challenge? Did you learn any new skills? Was there a time when you wondered if you would ever be able to achieve it? How did it feel when you did? Other questions such as 'What didn't you do that you could do next time?' can be used to stimulate thoughts and feelings.

This process shows that as unique, complex and sophisticated human beings we are continually developing and refining our skills throughout life, and that only through constant challenge, experience, action and reflection do we truly grow and evolve.

28

Nose Workout

Time: *10 mins*

Additional Resources: *2-6 small matchbox covers*

Teams pass a matchbox cover along the line using only their noses in a spirit of cooperation or competition

Divide the group into two or more teams – ideally eight to ten per team. Each team stands in a line with their hands behind their backs. Place a matchbox cover (a small one unless the children have incredibly large noses!) on the noses of the first player in each line. Each player passes the cover down the line, nose to nose. If it falls onto the floor, it is returned to the start of the line. The winning team is the first to pass the cover to the end.

Balloons can be substituted for matchbox covers but this method involves more personal areas of the body that aren't noses, and is therefore not suitable for all groups.

29

Body Scan

Time: *5 mins*

Additional Resources: *none*

Students practise mindfulness through this very relaxing, guided meditation. It can be performed while lying down, sitting, or standing but for classroom use, sitting is probably the best option.

Tell your students they're going to be learning a very powerful relaxation technique. When they're ready, read the following script...

Begin by closing your eyes if that's comfortable for you and take 3 slow deep breaths. With each out breath, feel your body relaxing more deeply.

In this exercise we're just going to bring our attention to our body from head to foot. That's all you have to do, just bring your attention to each area as I say it, as best you can.

We'll start at the very top of your head. See if you can notice how the crown of your head feels. See if you can just sense this area of your head.

Now bring your attention to the rest of your head and face – your forehead, your eyes, nose, mouth, the sides of your head and the back of your head. Just see if you can be aware of these parts of your body, noticing how these areas feel.

Notice your neck and your shoulders. If they feel tense or tight, allow them to soften.

Notice your chest and your upper back. Just get a sense for how these areas feel. And if there are any areas of tension or discomfort, just allow them to loosen and relax.

Notice your stomach and lower back.

Notice your arms, your hands and fingers.

Just sense these areas and let them loosen and relax.

Notice your back against the chair and the weight of your body on the chair.

Notice your legs, allowing them to loosen and relax.

Notice the sensations of your feet touching the floor. Sense the weight and pressure of your feet on the floor.

Now bring your attention to your whole body. Notice your whole body from head to toe and allow it to soften and relax more deeply.

Just enjoy this sense of relaxation as best you can, allowing any tense areas to soften further.

Take one more long slow, deep breath.

When you're ready, you can open your eyes.

30 Potato, Tights and a Balloon

Time: *10 mins*

Additional Resources: *a potato, a pair of tights and a balloon (per team)*

A totally daft game to develop the type of purposeless skill in which the British usually excel. Use sparingly!

The game involves swinging a potato dangling between the legs from a pair of tights tied around the waist. Two teams have to move a balloon across the room without using their hands or feet by swinging the potato. Depending on the surface, cheap footballs (smaller size) or small boxes may be more suitable than balloons.

This game could be varied but in essence it is meant to be fun. Just the introduction to this game, 'Today we're going to play a game involving ladies' tights, a potato and a balloon' will intrigue even the most battle-weary group of students. As with many of the 'energy' activities, this game won't be suitable for a group whose behaviour you find difficult to manage.

31

The Roll of the Die

Time: *5 mins*

Additional Resources: *1 die*

Students learn to summarise their learning following the roll of a die

This activity is best undertaken at the start or end of a session.

In groups students are asked to summarise a subject, topic or lesson in the number of sentences determined by the roll of the die. Each group throws the die separately. The die definitely adds to the excitement of this activity.

This technique works well following group discussions when table groups can summarise their discussion following the roll of the die.

32 Sitting Up Dead Lions

Time: *5 mins*

Additional Resources: *none*

Students explore relaxed and calm energy in a quiet game which can bond teacher and students

Calm down a group with this challenge. Ask everyone to be perfectly still and quiet. Then offer a prize to anyone who doesn't smile or laugh in the next two minutes. You then try to make everyone laugh by pretending to trip over, looking very closely at a child's face whilst pulling a silly expression, sharing some of your favourite jokes, reminiscing about a school trip or funny thing that happened in class. If you are not a teacher capable of making children smile either change job, enlist the help of a class member or dangle a tights-encased potato between your legs as you chase a balloon across the room.

There are usually a few children in every class who like to have fun and make others laugh. Usually considered disruptive, you are giving these children a chance to shine.

This is a version of one of the oldest games played between adults and children – the adult asking the child not to laugh and then making the child laugh. The title is not associated with the latest ill-fated England World Cup campaign.

33

Drinking Problem

Time: *5 mins*

Additional Resources: *8 matches and 1 penny coin*

Students have to solve a matchstick puzzle

Matches are arranged in the shape of two glasses (see illustration) and about 10 cm apart. Ask a class member to place the coin inside one of the cups. The other empty cup is only there to add to the confusion – it acts as a distraction because it looks like it must be part of the solution, when in fact it isn't.

The object of the puzzle is to get the coin out of the cup. The catch is you cannot touch the coin – you can only move two of the matches.

Now sit back smugly and enjoy the confusion.

For the solution to this grey cells confuddler, see diagram below.

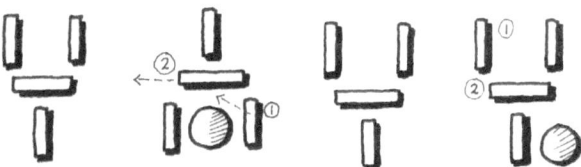

34 What Are You Looking At?

Time: *10 mins*

Additional Resources: *any objects you see fit or have to hand*

Students try eight ways of thinking, to discover how the most familiar, mundane things can become very interesting

It could be argued that everything is exciting if you look at it for long enough – it is just that a lot of us, either through our educational experiences or upbringing, stop looking. We start to develop apathy and rely on others to do the looking for us or for a teacher to just drop the photocopy into our laps.

So here's what you do. Pick an object such as a shoe. Then on the board write down these headings:

Numbers

Words

People

Feelings

Nature

Actions

Sights

Sounds

The students then brainstorm each of these areas as quickly as possible and write down as many connections as they can muster between 'shoe' and each heading. Before you know it, the groups will have created a veritable plethora of ideas, thoughts and connections. You can then invite the groups to feed back their findings to the class.

This activity uses a technique called 8 Way Thinking created by Ian Gilbert, the founder of Independent Thinking, to encourage students to look at things afresh and with a more discerning eye and to prove that everything is fascinating if only you look at it long enough.

35

Square Breathing

Time: *5–10 mins*

Additional Resources: *none*

Students practise a special breathing exercise to calm body and mind

The more interesting you can make an activity sound, the more likely your students will be to have a go at it. This breathing technique is used widely by the police, military and emergency services to help them remain calm in extremely stressful and traumatic situations –so it will be a really handy thing to practise this before a maths lesson.

When your students are ready, read the following script:

Breathe in slowly to a count of 4... 1, 2, 3, 4.

Now, hold your breath for another count of four... 1, 2, 3, 4.

Slowly breathe out for another count of 4... 1, 2, 3, 4.

Now you're going to hold your breath once again for another count of four... 1, 2, 3, 4.

Let's go through another cycle together:

Breathe in for four beats: 1, 2, 3, 4.

Hold your breath for four beats: 1, 2, 3, 4.

Breathe out for four beats: 1, 2, 3, 4.

And hold your breath for four beats: 1, 2, 3, 4.

Repeat this cycle another three or four times and ask students if they feel calmer.

36

The Lift

Time: *5 mins*

Additional Resources: *none*

Students explore trust and cooperation during this quick activity in which pairs of students standing back-to-back link arms and attempt to sit down and stand up again

Ask the group to line up from tallest to shortest. They pair up with the person they're standing beside (this ensures people of similar height are paired together). Standing back-to-back they link arms and have to sit down together and then stand up again. Stress that this is not a race – it is a test of teamwork, trust and communication skills.

If students complete the task twice, they'll find it easier the second time.

This activity shows that practice increases our level of performance. If they are asked to complete the task in silence the first time and can communicate during the second attempt, then lessons around the importance of communication will be made.

37

Show Business

Time: *15 mins*

Additional Resources: *pens and paper*

Students create a business from scratch

A statistic I read somewhere years ago claimed that the average student will have between ten and fourteen jobs, and within that, three to four different careers by the time they are 38 years old. I suspect it's far higher now. Factor into this that the majority of them will be self-employed in some capacity, then we can be certain of one thing: the world has most definitely changed and requires our younger generations to be more proactive, versatile and flexible than ever before.

Split students into groups and explain that the challenge is for them to create a business (you may wish to prepare these in advance to save time in the session). For instance, you could give one group an Italian restaurant, one a hairdresser, one an IT solutions company and one a mobile disco. They then must flesh out this business by answering questions such as:

What is your business/company name?

What is your mission statement?

How many people work for you?

What sort of people work for you?

How do you develop yourself/your staff?

Is your business local or global?

How many days/hours a week do you work?

What is your salary?

Does your company have a tagline or motto?

When they have done this the groups must feed back to the class. The students then decide which business they would or wouldn't invest in based on the ideas and information given.

This challenge creates an opportunity for the students to think about how to create a business and the questions they may need to ask themselves for it to become a reality.

38

Stare Off

Time: *5 mins*

Additional Resources: *none*

Students get to gaze into each other's eyes

My daughter Poppy loves this game and regularly challenges me to a contest across the breakfast table. The basic rules are this: on the command 'go' you must stare at your partner without blinking. That's it. You are also not allowed to distract each other.

You may, in a classroom environment, choose to do 'best of three' or get the winner of one pair to join the winner of another and keep joining groups until you have the best two left. They can then play the final in front of the class.

As well as being very funny this game is a great relationship builder as it requires students to stare at class members they may have ignored for three years.

39

Energy Escalator

Time: *10 mins*

Additional Resources: *none*

An energetic game in which individuals attempt to match a sequence of words with specific movements

A group is challenged to learn a sequence of movements associated with different forms of transport, for example:

Canoe (paddling action)

Plane (arms out like wings)

Car (holding steering wheel and moving it side to side)

Train (pull whistle)

Bungee (jump up and down three times)

Once these have been mastered, swap two of the movements around. Alternatively, use the game to demonstrate that we can learn more information if we add movements and fun to the learning process.

As an extension, and for even more fun, you can introduce sounds to accompany each action: Say 'splish splash' while canoeing, 'nnneeawwwww' while flying your plane, 'vroooom' while driving your car, 'choo choo' while pulling the train bell and 'arrrggghhhhhhh!' while bungee jumping.

40

Clap Together

Time: *5 mins*

Additional Resources: *none*

Students find out how in tune they are with their classmates by clapping

In pairs students attempt to clap in unison with their partner who must speed up and slow down without saying anything.

A more complex challenge is to ask students to clap their own hands together followed by clapping hands with their partner. If they are not in unison, it will quickly show.

Students can try this with a close friend and then someone they don't know as well. They are usually far more in tune with their friend. Did this happen in your group? Why?

Encourage students to improve their performance by developing concentration.

41

Plato's Cave

Time: *5 mins*

Additional Resources: *none*

This quick challenge is about what we notice around us, and it reveals much about how or what we see or don't see in life generally

Ask students to look around and make a list in thirty seconds of everything they see that is plastic.

Next ask students to close their eyes and write down from memory everything in the room that is metal. Their handwriting may not be neat but that's okay. Allow thirty seconds. The first list is usually much longer than the second.

Another version is to ask students to look at all the black objects in the room but then to write down all the green objects.

We always see more of what we're looking for or concentrating on. It's the reason we see loads of a particular type of car on the road, if we've decided we're going to buy one (you know, because of all that money teachers earn). It's the same throughout life. If we look for reasons to be sad or angry or happy, we will find plenty. It is not the world around us that determines our mood, it is something generated from within. Plato commented on this thousands of years ago. He suggested that we see life not as it is but as shadows reflected on a cave wall.

42

Hypno Sits

Time: *5 mins*

Additional Resources: *none*

Everyone gets to sit down (all at once) through intuition and a bit of witchcraft

It is always useful to have several techniques up your sleeve to calm a class and encourage focus. There is no point attempting to teach if half the class are still thinking about break time or what they just saw on TikTok.

Ask the entire class to stand up and face the front with their eyes closed. You then explain that only when the whole class is ready can everyone sit down as a group and at the same time. If people sit down at irregular intervals the game starts again. You may wish to try this out a few times with eyes open, so everyone gets comfortable with the idea.

What tends to happen is that for the first few attempts some students will be impatient and will try to force the sit, or others will get lost in a form of upright daydreaming. But if your group are working well together and are listening intently and sensing the mood of the room, you will on occasion have a moment where everyone is working together and en masse they sit down at the same time. When that happens you will be suspected of having special powers.

It is worth reminding ourselves that learning is not always just about the individual, it's also about the group; and when a group works well, great things can happen. This game forces the class to work as one and relies heavily on intuition and sensing the mood of the group.

43

Numbers in Letters

Time: *5 mins*

Additional Resources: *none*

Students are challenged to solve two puzzles which develop focus

Ask students to write out the numbers 1 to 10 in alphabetical order.

(Answer: eight, five, four, nine, one, seven, six, ten, three, two).

Ask students what number their name is by making each letter the value of its order in the alphabet (i.e. 1=a, 2=b etc, so David would be 40).

This kind of activity develops our capacity to quickly focus on the more complicated task that follows.

44

Well, I Never

Time: *5 mins*
Additional Resources: *none*
Students share stories

Any relationship gets better the more we feed it and share of ourselves. This activity allows students to share stories, facts and experiences with the class that they will not have heard before.

Announce to the class that they have two minutes to come up with a fact, story or experience that the class does not know about them. The student then feeds this back to the class.

Through sharing these experiences the groups get to discover new things about one another and perhaps common interests. More importantly they get to realise that everybody has a life outside of school and that everyone is different. It also proves that no matter how well you know a person, environment, situation or subject, with a little bit of curiosity and the right questions there will always be something new to discover.

Give it a whirl and see what you find out. The answers may surprise you.

45

Book Puzzle

Time: *5 mins*

Additional Resources: *none*

Students respond creatively to a conundrum

Ask your students: 'Why can't you hide a £10 note between pages 47 and 48 of a book with 300 pages?'

The 'real' answer is because books are laid out in a standard format with odd number pages on the right. But students usually have far more creative answers such as:

Because you don't have £10

Because the book doesn't have any numbers

Because the book only has 46 pages with numbers on and the rest are blank

Because the numbers have all been crossed out by someone in Year 9

Because you bought the book on Amazon and it's faulty

46

Copy That

Time: *5 mins*

Additional Resources: *none*

Students copy each other's work without being told off

This task can be difficult because of the requirement to maintain eye contact, which many adolescents find awkward and embarrassing, but it really is worth persevering. I did this activity once as part of a clown workshop. It was excruciating at first for an introvert like me, and yet incredibly rewarding.

In pairs students can either stand or sit opposite one another. One student is now A, and the other is B. Whilst maintaining eye contact student A can begin to move their arms and body (slowly at first). B's job is to mirror as exactly as possible A's movements. When this pattern has been established for long enough the roles can be swapped so B gets to lead.

Given that some teenagers spend hours in front of the mirror they should be really good at this.

47

In the Bin

Time: *2–5 mins*

Additional Resources: *1 bin, 1 tennis-size soft ball*

An energetic activity that gets the whole class on the move

This is one of the simplest competitive games to play and combines two techniques in one. First, throwing a ball to select students in a classroom environment is very useful for focus, concentration and hand-eye coordination, and also to ensure that the majority of students contribute and that it is not just the same two or three all the time.

Second, once the student has caught the ball (or it has ricocheted off them and hit three other students) you need to get the ball back. That's where the bin comes in.

You explain that on answering a question the student with the ball must now attempt to throw it into the bin. If the ball is successfully rehoused within the bin said student gets to leave before everyone else. If they miss they will remain seated until the bell, like the rest of the class, cosseted in the warm bosom of education.

You may be pleased to know that there is also a song to accompany this game. It is very easy to learn and in our experience adds to the drama. For your delectation we have included the words below. For best effect sing it to the tune of 'Ere we go! Ere we go! Ere we go!' (better known outside the football terrace as Sousa's Stars and Stripes Forever). 'Start it really slow and get faster and faster as the tension mounts.

In … the … bin

In the bin, in the bin, oi, oi

In the bin, in the bin, in the bin, oi, oi In the bin, in the bin, in the bin, oi, oi In the bi … in

In the bin.

Repeat until the ball has been lobbed into the bin.

This game works best with nothing other than 100% conviction and a little dollop of gusto.

48

Wing Man

Time: *5 mins*

Additional Resources: *none*

Students get to sneak a look at each other's work in a game of cooperation and stealth

This activity is a splendid way to review a lesson or to find out how much a group already knows.

You can split up the class into groups or pairs. For the sake of explaining we'll use pairs. Between them they designate who will be the pilot (i.e. in charge and who writes down all the information) and who will be the wingman (i.e. the scout who will fly missions to other tables to gain intel, ideas and knowledge that can then be debriefed back at HQ, i.e. their table).

This is a lively way to get the students to do all the legwork and encompasses some of the key elements of this book – energy, connection and focus.

49

Five Senses

Time: *5 mins*

Additional Resources: *none*

Students are invited to practise mindful awareness by tuning in fully to their surroundings

The Five Senses Exercise as a simple way to evoke a calm, more mindful state using the five senses.

Ask your students to sit quietly and take three slow, deep calming breaths. Then read the following script...

Notice five things that you can see.

Without turning your head, look around the room in front of you and bring your attention to five things you might not normally notice. Choose something you wouldn't ordinarily pay attention to, like a shadow or a small hole in the wall.

Notice four things that you can feel.

Now bring your attention to four things you are currently feeling, like the texture of your clothes, the pressure of your feet on the floor, the weight of your body on the chair, the feeling of the air on your face, or the surface of the table you are resting your hands on.

Notice three things that you can hear.

Try to tune in to the sounds of your surroundings. What can you hear in the background? This might be the faint sounds of traffic from a nearby road, the noise from other classrooms, the hum of a computer or a clock ticking.

Notice two things that you can smell.

Tune your senses into smells you might not normally notice. Perhaps the smell of your clothes, or perfume, or the smell of books.

Notice one thing that you can taste.

Focus on one thing you can taste right now, in this moment. Maybe you can taste saliva in your mouth, some remnants of food from earlier or perhaps you could open your mouth to search the air for a taste.

Remember that this type of exercise becomes easier the more it is practised. And it's through regular practice of mindfulness exercises like this that the real benefits are experienced.

50 A Golden Ticket for Life

Time: *5 mins*

Additional Resources: *three sheets of paper (preferably a golden colour and in the shape of a star)*

One or more students win an unexpected prize in a game of random luck rather than skill – the format currently favoured by so many TV shows

Before the lesson starts, randomly place one, two or three golden tickets (or yellow A4 sheets divided into squares – sorry to ruin the magic) under chair seats. (Prepare yourself for some shocking – and potentially hazardous – finds beneath some chairs). If your students always sit at the same seats, ask them all to move for this lesson. This in itself is an interesting exercise and an insight into our human nature to avoid change.

Build up a little tension and excitement by asking students to imagine what it would be like to win a lottery. What would be the best prize? Health, wealth, love, fame?

Reveal that there are winners in this class. Some people will be very successful. Then ask students to look under their seats to see who has won.

Ask the winning students to share their hopes and ambitions with the class. If this ticket meant they could have the life they desired, what would they choose? Classmates could be encouraged to offer encouragement and ideas on how the winners could be their best.

Don't we all like the idea of winning something for doing little or nothing?

A raffle win can bring far greater excitement than is justified by the jar of kumquats in fruit liqueur once presented to us by the smiling elderly lady who had organised the tombola. Why is it we win back a prize less useful and valuable than the contribution we made ourselves? In life the reality is that occasionally, but only very occasionally, we do win prizes for doing nothing. But for the most part, effort is rewarded (doh!).

I was recently told a story about a man who approached a well-known shampoo manufacturer and said he could double their sales with just one word. He offered to share it for a million pounds. He was paid on the condition (or conditioner?) it worked. The word was 'repeat' added to the instructions on the back of the shampoo bottle. Although it didn't double sales it did result in enough people washing their hair twice instead of once to ensure he was paid handsomely for his efforts. Not quite something for nothing, but not a bad return on an idea that must have flashed into his consciousness in less than a second.

I've no way of verifying this story but I hope you'll agree it's a good one, and it does get the cogs turning in your Year 10 groups' heads (shampooed or not).

51

Future Intros

Time: *10 mins*

Additional Resources: *none*

Students get to meet their future self

I often wonder what it would be like to meet myself in the future (this is what happens when you don't have any friends). What would I be like? What would I be doing?

Give the students five minutes to think about and make notes on their future selves (let's say twenty years in the future). Ask them to flesh out this person in as much detail as possible.

Then in turn each member of the class must walk to the front and introduce themselves to the group as their future self. The structure below is a good one to follow for the basic introduction.

Good morning/afternoon.

My name is … and I am … years old. I live in (insert country or town here).

I am a (insert profession here). The best thing about my job is …

I could never have achieved this without … Knowing what I know now I wish I had … when I was at school.

Thanks for listening. Bye.

This activity works wonders for confidence and gives the students permission to rehearse their success and feel what it is like to be doing the things they dream of doing. As an add- on you may wish to experiment with a couple of ridiculous intros first to build up class confidence. Why don't you give it a bash now and see where you are in ten or twenty years' time?

This game gives the students an opportunity to introduce their future self to the group.

52 Stand Up, Sit Down, Sit Up, Stand Down

Time: *5 mins*

Additional Resources: *none*

Students get to do exactly what it says on the tin

We love games that are designed to make your brain hurt and this is one of them. It is much like Simon Says and is a quick way to get the class moving, laughing and in a flap. The actions speak for themselves but for the sake of argument we'll explain them anyway:

When you say 'stand up' the class stand up.

When you say 'sit down' the class sit down – they must sit slumped in their chair as if they are in the most boring lesson of all (not yours, of course).

When you say 'sit up' the class must sit bolt upright wearing the expression of a happy and over-enthusiastic learner (we can all hope).

When you say, 'stand down' everyone puts their hands up and shouts 'It wasn't me'.

The fun comes from mixing up the order of instructions or creating a pattern that the students get familiar with only to change it at the last second.

A great way to get the blood pumping and to oxygenate the brain, either at the beginning or midway through a session.

53
Mindful colouring

Time: *10-15 mins*

Additional Resources: *Mandala colouring sheets or similar*

A quick calming activity to lower the energy of a group and promote focus

This could be seen as something of a copout by some teachers, but I've always found it to have a wonderfully calming influence – on adults and kids alike.

Stick on some relaxing music (or whale noises if you prefer), light an incense stick and give your group ten minutes to lose themselves in some relaxing colouring-in activity. It's perfect for a cooling off period, a registration activity or as a calming starter prior to more taxing work.

54

Chocolate Boxes

Time: *10 mins preparation, then 5 minutes in the classroom*

Additional Resources: *3 boxes (shoe boxes are ideal), 3 chocolate bars and 3 labels (slips of paper will be adequate)*

Students think 'inside the box' to think outside of the box in this mental puzzle

Three boxes contain one chocolate bar each: a Mars, Crunchie and Wispa. They are labelled 'Mars', 'Crunchie' and 'Mars or Crunchie'. All three labels are wrong. How many boxes do you need to open in order to make all the labels correct?

Answer: none. The box labelled 'Mars or Crunchie' must contain the Wispa. Therefore the box labelled 'Mars' must contain the Crunchie and the label 'Crunchie' must contain the Mars. Try it out – it works!

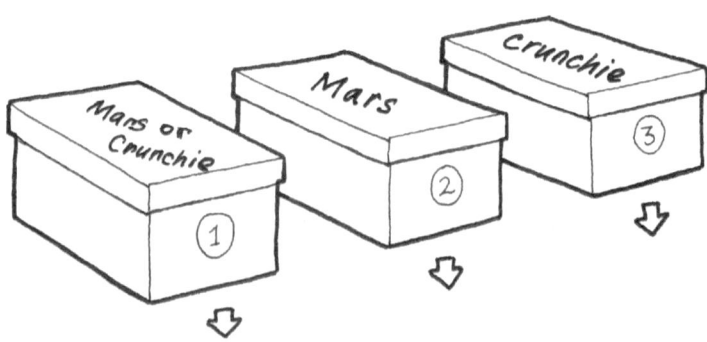

A game that has the potential for students to be rewarded with chocolate tends to be very popular.

55 Alphabetti Never Forgetti

Time: *5 mins*

Additional Resources: *none*

Students get twenty-six keywords from a lesson

Revision is not an option, and you can never have enough ways to review a lesson. This is a good one as it requires the students to think of specific words rather than just say the same thing as their mate or other phrases like, 'It was alright', 'I dunno' and 'Can I have my headphones back?'

With five minutes to go, announce that you are going to review the lesson using the letters of the alphabet. As you go around the class each student must then come up with a word that starts with the corresponding letter of the alphabet they are given.

The word can either have been mentioned during the lesson or is in some way feedback regarding the lesson. Random words are not allowed even if they start with the right letter.

This technique promotes quick thought and encourages all the students to contribute to the summing up of a lesson.

56

Building Memory

Time: *10 mins*

Additional Resources: *none*

Recreate a classic method for remembering stuff using your students as VAK (visual, auditory and kinaesthetic) models

Nominate six to nine people to share a different fact or statement with the whole group. This could be six to nine different key points about your subject or random personal information to illustrate the point of this activity (we remember information better if it is made memorable in VA K systems). They could stand at the front if this is a large class activity or could work in groups of six to eight spread around the room. Each person shares their fact in sequence. Repeat this three or four times. Part way through the next sequence ask for the group to predict/remember the next fact in line.

Don't worry about a few wrong answers because, once clarified, these are even more likely to be remembered next time. It helps if facts are delivered in memorable ways, such as with funny accents or whilst adopting a body posture linked to the fact.

This activity works well with subjects or topics that have sequences of information that need to be learned and remembered. For example, seven students could each deliver a feature of life.

57

Heavy Breathing

Time: *5–10 mins*

Additional Resources: *none*

Students practise the way humans have learned to focus their attention by simply being aware of and controlling their breathing rate

Although we've all learned how to breathe – it is one of the first things we learn and it is something we've done all our lives – like many habits it is an unconscious action. Until we think about it, like now.

Be aware of your breathing now. There's amazing chemistry in your lungs exchanging gases; amazing biology feeding millions of cells with energy and life-giving oxygen. It really is amazing. If you're 15 you've probably breathed in 240 million times (and breathed out exactly the same number of times – we can put the numbers out of sync by breathing in twice but out only once on our next breath). The sequence we learn is in-out, in-out for breathing. There are exceptions. When we cry, we generally breathe in a few times for each out breath.

As a quick experiment ask students, whilst breathing at their normal rate, to see how many in-breaths they can take without breathing out. Most people manage around six. This gives us an idea of the amount of lung capacity we use at rest – perhaps one sixth, or about 16%. This is a good metaphor for life in general; we use only a fraction of our full potential.

The next part of the activity is basically a relaxation exercise:

Breathe in through your nose for a count of three then hold for six seconds

Breathe out slowly through your mouth for a count of six seconds

Repeat three times

On each in-breath ask the group to imagine breathing in fresh, clean air and visualise it filling their lungs and body with energy and power to be their best today. As they hold their breath, ask them to imagine all that energy and power spreading through their entire body. On each out-breath they should release tension and negative thoughts from wherever they are in the body, draining them away till they're gone.

Ask students to focus on the lesson ahead and what they are about to learn.

This type of breathing technique has been used for thousands of years across many cultures and can be very useful in the classroom to relax students and get them in a better state for learning.

58 Semi-Supine and the Schwa

Time: *10 mins*

Additional Resources: *none*

Students get to lie down and make noises in a productive and focused manner

This activity draws directly from the Alexander technique, a method of managing change through the symbiosis of body and mind which was formulated by Frederick Matthias Alexander (1869–1955).

Students need to be lying down on their backs with their knees bent up facing the ceiling and in line with their hips.

They must place their hands just under their ribs (which is directly on top of the diaphragm).

Ask them to close their eyes and concentrate on their breathing as this will help them to become relaxed yet alert.

Ask them to breathe in for four counts, and to feel their ribs moving out across the floor, and out for four counts until every last bit of air has gone, all the while making sure they remain as relaxed as possible. Repeat this activity several times.

Some students may find this awkward or are more concerned with what everyone else is up to, but it is worth persevering to get the group into the correct state. Over time and with practice the students will relax into this very quickly.

Once the correct state has been established you can introduce the next phase. This time ask the students to take a deep breath, allow their jaw to relax and drop open, and then release one long sustained 'AAAAAAAAAAAAAAAAH' sound. If they are creating the sound from the right place (i.e. their diaphragm) the noise will be relaxed and open. If they are tense it will sound trapped and will cause tension in the throat.

Phonetically, the clear open sound emitted is called a schwa. All this work enables students to begin developing breath control which is essential in the management of stress and the ability to remain calm and access the thinking brain when the going gets tough.

59

One-Liners

Time: *5 mins*

Additional Resources: *1 piece of paper*

Students create a story in two minutes

Start off with a piece of paper with 'Once upon a time...' written at the top. You pass this to the first student who writes the next line. When they have completed their line they must fold over the top of the paper (covering up 'Once upon a time...') and only leaving their line exposed. Let this process continue around the class so that each time someone contributes a line they can only see and respond to the line written before and nothing else.

Before you know it, you'll have a story and probably a bizarre one at that. You can then choose someone to read it whilst the rest of the group marvel at the wonder of it all.

Openness is the key to creativity and in this activity it is given free rein.

60 Here the Drummer Gets Wicked

Time: *5 mins*

Additional Resources: *none*

Students get to make noise and feel what it is like to be in the moment

My lifelong passion is drumming. I've had periods of my life during which a drum kit hasn't been present in my house, but I always have a pair of sticks close to hand and find something to tap on. For this activity you need neither drums nor sticks – you can either clap or use a desk to create the beat. You can use pretty much anything.

You will need to be the conductor, so begin by establishing a basic beat to the count of four like the one below (beat = clap or tap on the desk, number = count or nod silently):

Beat Beat 3 4

Beat Beat 3 4

Beat Beat 3 4

Once this has been established you can, as the conductor, raise the volume by bringing your right hand upwards or decrease volume by bringing your right hand downwards. If the group are focusing on the beat, you shouldn't even need to explain the volume signals, they will just follow you.

When you begin to feel more confident you can start to play around with different rhythms and patterns like the ones below:

Beat 2 Beat 4

Or

Beat Beat Beat 4

Or

Beat 2 Beat Beat

Or if you're feeling really cocky you can double-time it like this:

Beat Beat Beat Beat Beat Beat Beat Beat

You can also add another element here which is to split the room into two so that one side are playing one rhythm whilst the other side are playing a different one. Splitting the room into four means you can practically build an amazing wall of sound that will make other classes wish they were in your lesson.

When you really get into drumming it becomes a marvellous exercise in preset moment awareness; you can only ever be in the moment and it's impossible to think of anything else other than what you are drumming. It's an amazingly effective way to focus the mind, bringing everything you are doing into the now, and in the context of this exercise it really galvanises the group to work together, making it a tremendous way to connect.

This also confirms what many punitive teachers have thought for years – if you beat something hard enough you can produce great results!

61

Moon Walking

Time: *20–30 mins (this activity could be split into two parts over consecutive lessons)*

Additional Resources: *copy sheets 1 and 2 (below) for each student*

Students are asked to rank a series of supplies following an emergency landing of their spacecraft on the moon. First, they work alone and then in a group. Will everyone survive?

I loved my time in the outdoor activity world, delivering corporate team-building days. Many of the indoor training activities we offered were generally rather tedious but a few were both enjoyable and instructive. The following activities are two of the best.

Invite your students to believe they have been selected to be the first group of students from earth to take part in an exchange visit with a school on Mars. Sadly, on the way to Mars their space bus makes an emergency landing on the moon. You are sixty miles from the rescue station on the light side of the moon. All equipment has been destroyed except spacesuits and the ten items listed below.

The game has two parts. First, individually they must rank the items from 1 to 10 in order of importance for survival. Answers to be written in column I. Second, they agree a ranking in their groups or the whole class. Answers to be written in column G.

Supply each student with sheet 1.

The group is then given sheet 2 and asked to transfer their previous ranking scores onto this sheet:

Sheet 1

Rank these items in order, most important 1 to least important 10

	1 (Individual's Score)	G (Group Score)
Supply of water for each person		
Oxygen-filled tanks		
Map of moon showing route to destination		
Food concentrate		
Box of matches		
Parachute silk		
Magnetic compass		
First aid kit		
Solar powered heater		
50 feet of nylon rope		

Sheet 2

	Nasa rank	I Score	Diff N I	Nasa rank	G Score	Diff N I
Supply of water	2					
Oxygen tanks	1					
Moon map	3					
Food concentrate	4					
Box matches	10					
Parachute silk	7					
Compass	9					
First aid kit	5					
Solar powered heater	8					
Nylon rope	6					
Total Diff						

You can download printable versions of these sheets from our website here:

www.needsfocusedteaching.com/changemood-resources

Group discussion

First, each person records on sheet 2 the numerical difference between each individual ranking and the NASA ranking. For example: if oxygen is ranked 3 by the individual and 1 by NASA, the difference is 2. Total up all 10 and record at the bottom of the sheet.

If your score is low, you did well and stand a good chance of survival should you ever visit the moon. Also record the difference between your group rankings and NASA's. Was your individual ranking total score lower (and therefore closer to NASA's scientists) than your group ranking score? If so, you were open to be persuaded by group members, so much so that your better answers were disregarded by the group! If your group score was closer to NASA's than your individual score, then your openness helped improve your performance.

Sometimes in life we are open to other people's ideas and suggestions and sometimes we stick to our own opinions. Neither is always right or always wrong. Knowing when to be open to new ideas and when to stick to our own ideas is one of the most difficult things to learn.

NASA scientists agreed the rankings based on their knowledge of the moon as follows:

1. Oxygen: essential for survival.

2. Water: next most important for survival.

3. Map: required to locate base.

4. Food concentrate: required for energy.

5. First aid kit: important should anyone have an accident.

6. Nylon rope: useful for climbing cliffs and tying injured people together.

7. Parachute silk: useful protection from sun.

8. Solar powered heater: only needed on dark side of moon.

9. Compass: a magnetic compass would work on earth but would be useless on the moon.

10. Matches are worthless as there is no oxygen on the moon to light a match.

62 Ready, Steady, Draw

Time: *15–25 mins*

Additional Resources: *copy sheets 1 and 2 (below) for each pair of students*

Students discover the importance of clear instructions in a drawing game

Students work in pairs for this activity. Sitting back-to-back works well, as does a screen separating both students.

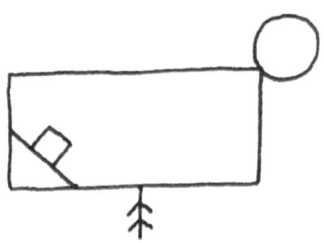

The idea is that one student describes the diagram above for their partner to draw. The partner doing the drawing does not see the template diagram until after they have finished. The describer does not see the drawing as it is being drawn. A three-minute time limit helps ensure the diagram and the drawing have as little in common as a teenage boy and a bar of soap. Swap over for a second attempt using the second illustration. This time you'll probably find much more attention being given to the quality of instruction, and the accuracy increasing dramatically.

At the end of the activity students share their experiences.

The learning point is the importance of good, clear communication.

63

I'm Changing

Time: *5 mins*

Additional Resources: *none*

Students learn without realising that change is uncomfortable

In an ever-changing world, and especially one in which technology evolves ever faster and life and work are more interchange able and flexible, it is imperative that our young folk embrace and manage change – to be at the forefront of it so they can leave school and not just cope with life but fully engage with it.

Split the students up into pairs. Each pair must observe the other for about sixty seconds, paying particular attention to how the other looks and what they are wearing. Once they have done this they must both turn back-to-back and change three things about their appearance. For instance, they may take off a watch, undo a tie or slip off a shoe – but if the group is especially boisterous you may have to discourage a full striptease!

Once the three changes have been made the pair can face each other and then hazard a guess as to what changes each other has made. When they have done this they can sit down. When everyone has sat down you can then pose these five questions:

1. Who guessed all three changes?

2. Who guessed two?

3. Who guessed one?

4. Who didn't guess any?

5. Who has put, or is in the process of putting, back what they originally changed?

This last question is fundamental, as 99% of the group will have immediately put everything back as it was. You can then explain that this game is an analogy for change. Sometimes change can be fun, uncomfortable, interesting or a bit weird, but at the end of the day we much prefer to slip back into our old ways of doing things.

We are creatures of habit and stick to our routines even if we know they are bad for us or are hindering our progress. All change is unnerving but only through courage, confidence and constant application can we hope to grow and accomplish the things we want to achieve.

As an alternative, the teacher can be the one making the changes. I remember a trainer using this exercise throughout a whole training day I was attending. He made small changes to his appearance without warning and then every 20 minutes or so he'd stop and ask the delegates what was different. It's one of the few times I've seen a trainer enjoy 100% attention from attendees throughout an entire day.

This game works as an analogy for change and is very effective.

64

Big Brother

Time: 5 mins

Additional Resources: none

Students have the chance to look at the choices they make and whether they are the right ones

The answers you get to this question can be eye-opening to say the least. The question is this: if you were being watched all the time, what wouldn't you do?

My list was too long to publish but suffice to say I realised that I have several habits that need some immediate attention!

A useful way to deploy this question is to have it already written up on the board as the students come in.

65

Missing Letters

Time: 5 mins

Additional Resources: a random paragraph of text either on screen or paper

Students are given a challenge to measure their ability to switch focus from the specific to the broad and back again

Give students a random paragraph of text and ask them to circle every 's'. Ask them to go back and see if they missed any. They usually do! You can repeat the challenge a few times using the same text. Perhaps ask a question based on comprehension the second time such as, 'What colour was the hat?'

This simple activity demonstrates the narrow way in which we tend to focus our attention at school (focus/convergent thinking). The opposite is divergent thinking/openness. Both are useful.

66 How Many Triangles?

Time: *5 mins*

Additional Resources: *copy of illustration (below) on interactive board or on paper*

A quick puzzle to focus the attention of a group

Draw out or display the following shape and ask the students to count the number of triangles.

Answer: 27.

67

Tattoo Review

Time: *5 mins*

Additional Resources: *none*

A great review activity in which students learn that body art can be educational

With five minutes before the end of the session, announce that the students must come up with an image or word that best sums up the lesson. They are then to draw said word or image on the back of their hands as a reminder of the key point.

This is a really useful way to get students to reflect on their learning because later on they may be doing something completely unrelated and by chance catch a glimpse of the word or may even be questioned about it by a friend or family member.

68

An Open Exam

Time: 10 mins

Additional Resources: copy exam paper (below) for each student

Students attempt an exam with a difference. Will they spot the 'trick'?

Copy and distribute the following exam sheet to each student. State that they must work under exam conditions and have five minutes to finish. Say that you expect every student to answer all six questions correctly.

This is an activity demonstrating the value of looking carefully at the detail and reading through all of the instructions before starting – a great exercise to share just before exams. This activity was inspired by the book The Mysterious Benedict Society by Trenton Lee Stewart.

In life the answers are all around us. It is just a question of whether we see the answers by looking anew at familiar things.

Exam Sheet

Read all questions before answering.

1　Which of the following is the correct spelling of the condition caused by the recessive gene passed on in the X chromosome?
a. haemophilia
b. **haemaphilia**
c. haemophilia

2　In 1940 the evacuation of Dunkirk saved how many soldiers?
a. **33,000**
b. 165,000
c. **330,000**

3　The cube of a number (X³) is the number multiplied by itself three times (e.g. 3 x 3 x 3 = 27). What is the cube of 4?
a. 16
b. **64**
c. **400**

4　Haemophilia is passed on through which chromosome?
a. X
b. Y
c. Z

5　In what year did the evacuation of Dunkirk rescue **330,000** soldiers?
a. 1940
b. 1942
c. 1944

6　If the cube of 4 is **64** what is the cube 3?
a. 9
b. **27**
c. 81

You can download printable versions of these sheets from our website here:

69 Peer Inspiration Project

Time: *5 mins followed up in short inputs of up to 5 mins per lesson for 1 or more lessons*

Additional Resources: *none*

Students derive inspiration from their peers

Few things inspire teenagers more than seeing their peers succeed. Witnessing someone 'just like me' achieve success is a powerful motivator. Look through regional newspapers and collect examples of local children demonstrating qualities such as bravery, loyalty, hard work, altruism and so on.

As a challenge you could ask students to mirror this approach in a simple way by researching local people demonstrating admirable qualities. This could be from their own families or communities. As a step-up you could invite previous students back into school to be interviewed by current students.

This exercise links into Better than the Oscars (Activity 77).

70

Initially Speaking

Time: *5 mins*

Additional Resources: *paper/sticky notes, pens*

A quick way to review lesson content

With five minutes before the end of the session get the students to use their initials to come up with a useful phrase or set of keywords from the lesson. They can then feed these back to the class.

Get the class to jot their answers down on paper/sticky notes so you can put them on the wall, and with little or no effort you have an instant lesson check and informative display for your wall.

71

Spot the Deference

Time: *10-20 mins*

Additional Resources: *paper and pens*

Students get to explore and reflect on the value of respect

In our dealings with young people the word 'respect' crops up regularly and can often be the catalyst for good or bad behaviour.

Ask the class to write down the word 'respect' in the centre of a piece of paper and then add anything that comes to mind which directly relates to their thoughts and feelings about the word.

You may wish to use the technique 'What Are You Looking At?' (Activity 34) to really flesh out this process.

When they have done this, they can feed back their findings. You can further the debate by asking if anyone can give an example of an experience where they have felt respected or disrespected. How did it make them feel? How did they feel about the other person? What didn't they do? What could they do next time?

Next, ask the students to think of someone they respect and list five reasons why. As a group it is interesting to amalgamate the results to find any common threads. Then ask the group what it means to have respect in oneself and feedback these answers.

When all this information has been gathered it may be very useful to put together a list of the things you must do to get respect. This can be put up on the wall for everyone to see and as a constant reminder that to get respect, you've got to give it.

72

Story Time

Time: *5–10 mins*

Additional Resources: *none*

In small groups students are given a 7-word story (title: 1 word; story: 6 words) and are asked to make sense of it

Split students into small groups and ask:

What's going on?

What do you know after reading the story?

What assumptions can you make when you read the following story?

The story:

Title: Monsters

Story: They knew they needed to move.

The learning point is that when we are open to new ideas, there are infinitely more possibilities.

For example: 'they' could be monsters considering a move, or could be creatures seeking to move away from (or toward) the monsters; there could be one or more groups of varying sizes (family, tribe, planet); and 'move' could mean move home, place of work, bodies, possessions and so on.

73 The Aliens Have Landed

Time: *10–15 mins*

Additional Resources: *none*

Students have to argue the case for the survival of the human race to an intergalactic group of aliens

The groups are asked to imagine that an alien delegation has landed on earth and each group of students is asked to plead for the human race to join an intergalactic group of worthy species. How would they present their case? What positive qualities do humans possess? Which of these qualities do group members possess? When are humans at their best?

Groups of students get to focus on and discuss positive human qualities.

74

Friends Reunited

Time: *every 10 mins*

Additional Resources: *none*

A brilliant speed dating-type review activity

Get the students to learn kinaesthetically by requesting that every ten minutes they must move to the next seat in a clockwise motion and then share what they have learnt during the lesson.

In a typical fifty-minute lesson the students will have to review the content five times, which is more than enough to strengthen the synaptic connections in the brain and lay down clear neural path- ways for future use.

75 Chewing Gum Stretch

Time: *5 mins*

Additional Resources: *none (don't worry – not even chewing gum!)*

Students get to do a physical warm-up using the chewing gum of their choice

This is a brilliant energizer.

Ask the students to stand up and to imagine they are chewing a big piece of gum. Encourage them to really enjoy chewing and moving it around in their mouth. Then suggest they blow bubbles with it – the bigger the better – until it bursts. Now suggest they bite the chewing gum between their teeth and pull outwards as far as they can, maybe wrapping it around all of their fingers. Then they should take the gum out of their mouth and begin to stretch it in all directions.

Ask them to pull it apart as far as it will go and then see if they can get their left leg over the top, then the right leg. Now suggest they roll it up into a ball and throw it to the ground by their feet. They should stand on the gum and try to lift up their right leg and then their left. Remind them that it is really sticky and strong.

You get the idea – you can play around with this concept all day as long as it enables the students to have a good stretch and a good laugh.

This is a wonderfully creative way to get students to stretch and physically warm themselves up without realising it.

76 Soap Opera Moments

Time: *5 mins*

Additional Resources: *none, or prepare cards using the headings/categories below (this will take only 5 mins)*

A comedy improvisation game

Groups are given a genre of storytelling and a scenario to act out in the genre presented. The more random and bizarre the combination the better the results.

Sample genres include: romance, comedy, horror, action/thriller, sci-fi, children's TV, wildlife documentary.

Sample scenes include: X Factor auditions, taking a pet to the vet, a hospital visit, football match, school canteen.

77 Better than the Oscars

Time: *5 mins to introduce, follow-up of 2–5 mins per award*

Additional Resources: *award certificates/ trophies if required*

Students are invited to introduce a rewards system more effective than being paid money

The teacher should consider the logistics within the group before they introduce this activity. Factors such as how often you see the class are important. You could always let your group decide the best way to introduce the idea.

Set up a system for peers to award peers with certificates (for added prestige they could take the form of Oscars, or a format suggested by the students). They could be based on values agreed by your class or the whole school such as kindness, respect or humour. Control and ownership should be with the students, so teachers need to avoid awarding the certificates. They will mean more when received from their peers.

Rules should include that the awards/certificates must be made on the day of the positive act (or as near to it as agreed by the group as realistic) and the giver must present it in class with a short explanation.

This idea is based on a similar system adopted by an engineering company in the US and described in Drive by Daniel Pink; but there are plenty of similar results. In a town in the US 50% of residents were asked if they would accept a nuclear reprocessing plant in their neighbourhood by appealing to their sense of civic responsibility. The other 50% were asked the same question but in addition were offered a sum of money equal to 10% of their annual salary to accept the reprocessing plant. Which group were more likely to agree to the plant? What do you think? It was the first group by a significant margin. Money is not the best motivator in many areas of people's lives.

78

Tableau for Four

Time: 5–10 mins

Additional Resources: none

A review activity in which students get to create still images of the lesson

Towards the end of the lesson explain that the class are going to review the lesson in groups of four. They will do this by creating four different snapshots of the session. Everyone in the group must take part and they have five minutes to come up with the goods, and five minutes to present the snapshots back to the group.

As an added extra the students could photograph the tableaux and load them onto the class computer where they could be presented as a slideshow.

This is a super way to ensure that everyone gets involved in the revision process and not just the confident ones who love an audience.

79

Spellbound

Time: *10 mins*

Additional Resources: *none*

A review activity in which students spell out keywords without saying a word

If you want to get the students to work together and find new ways to communicate other than speaking, this is a great game to start with.

Before the lesson think of some of the keywords that you would most like the students to remember when they leave. Decide on group numbers (depending on the length of your longest keyword). The students then have one minute to spell out the word using only their bodies. Strictly no talking!

This process helps the students to focus, be open and above all develop their muscle memory. If you have a particularly large group which likes a challenge, then get them to spell out the word below as a warm-up:

HONORIFICABILITUDINITATIBUS

According to 'QI' this is apparently the longest word used by Shakespeare (in Love's Labour's Lost) and means 'the quality of deserving honour or respect'.

80

Story Wheel

Time: *15 mins*

Additional Resources: *none*

Students revolve and evolve their creative muscles in this storytelling gem

For this activity you may need to move all desks to the side of the room. A good bit of cardiovascular never hurt anyone.

The students, each sitting on a chair, need to create an inner circle A and an outer circle B. The B's must now begin a story, which can be about anything but to make it slightly more interesting and challenging you explain that their story must involve a carrot (or anything else you decide).

Allow the B's to continue for a couple of minutes then shout 'stop'. The A's must now move around one place, so they are opposite someone different. A's must now repeat back to their new partner the story so far but this time, when continuing the story, A's must now add in a submarine (or any other random object/thought) to further the narrative.

This continues for a few minutes and then the A's move around again, the B's must repeat back what they have just heard, and in their retelling must mention something new and bizarre. And so on and so on.

When you feel that this activity has come to a natural end it is always worth listening to a couple of the stories to see how different and disturbing they turned out.

This activity works on many levels and encourages the students to think fast, incorporate new ideas and information, listen well, communicate and deal with new people – as well as being as imaginative as possible.

81

Human Magnets

Time: *5 mins*

Additional Resources: *none*

Students get stuck to everything in a fast-paced warmup

This is another great game to get students physically warmed up and ready for learning. You can have as much fun as you want with this but you may wish to start off small and build it up.

Get the students on their feet and announce to the group that due to a bizarre accident in the canteen, and the release of unidentified gases, their index fingers are now magnetic and are for some unknown reason attracted to their noses. On this remark you must quickly put your finger on your nose, so the class follow. Now, try as you might, you cannot pull your finger from your nose. The harder you pull the stronger the connection.

Your finger then gets attracted to the back of your knee and then to the back of someone else's knee. Then your left elbow suddenly becomes magnetic and is attracted to a desk (whilst your index finger is still stuck hard and fast to the back of someone's leg). Then your whole body becomes magnetised and is compelled to get attached to one corner of the room. This one is brilliant to watch as everyone rushes into the corner of the room and cannot move. You get the idea.

The fun comes from playing around with the notion of attracting one body part to anything else in the room that causes the students to stretch themselves mentally and physically.

82 Remote Voice Control

Time: *10 mins*

Additional Resources: *none*

Students get to control each other vocally in an activity to develop focus and communication

Split the class in half and have them standing in two lines facing each other so that everyone has somebody opposite them (about two feet apart).

The first part of the activity looks at communication and how we do it. Let the pairs decide who is A and who is B.

A's start first by saying a chosen line to B (such as a line from Shakespeare's Romeo and Juliet: 'Two households both alike in dignity').

Try saying it two feet apart and then gradually increase the distance between the A's and B's by getting the A's to take a step back after each utterance of the line.

When both A and B have had a go, discuss with the group what they noticed whilst speaking and watching. What did they do vocally and physically the further they moved away and vice versa?

The next phase is to give the A's control over the B's. Below are signals that A can use to control how B delivers the line:

1. The pitch is controlled by moving the right hand up (pitch is higher) and down (pitch is lower).

2. Volume is controlled by moving the right hand from left to right (far left means quiet, far right means as loud as possible).

3. Speed is controlled by pretending you have a fishing rod. The quicker you reel it in the faster your partner must speak. The slower you reel it in the slower your partner must speak.

Allow the students to have as much fun as they can with this and watch as they develop their vocal dexterity, focus and communication.

83 May the Force Be With You

Time: 5–10 mins

Additional Resources: none

Optional: show a clip from www.ted.com suitable for older groups

Students are challenged to consider how best to influence people

This activity is inspired by advertiser Rory Sutherland's talks (available to view on www.ted.com). There is a myth that greater force results in greater influence.

For example, speed cameras are often in the news, and they divide public opinion. Drivers caught speeding face the threat of a fine, penalty points on their licence, and even a driving ban. The more recent smiley or sad face signs which flash as motorists pass accident black-spots are only 10% of the cost of speed cameras and carry no penalty.

Which do you think has the greater influence on driver behaviour? It is the face – twice as effective as speed cameras at reducing driver speed.

Another example is from Prussia a few hundred years ago. Leader Frederick the Great wanted his people to adopt the potato as part of their diet. He reasoned that with two basic food crops – grain (to create flour for bread) and the potato

– his subjects would be less susceptible to famine because if one crop failed the other would come to the rescue.

The problem he had was that people hated the potato so much that even passing a law compelling people to grow and eat potatoes proved ineffective. His solution was to decree the potato a royal food only available to the elite. The imperial spuds were guarded by his finest soldiers, but he secretly told them to guard the crop badly. Once the peasants thought of the potato in this new way its popularity soared. (The other thing he could have done was to invent chips, of course.)

Challenge your group to think in an open way about other problems and potential solutions. For example, how to encourage the wearing of school uniform or how to get people to adopt kinder behaviour or become more green. Sutherland suggests making gas-guzzling cars compulsory for convicted criminals thus making them unpopular.

84

Walkabout

Time: *5 mins*

Additional Resources: *none*

A punchy and effective warm-up game

Clear a space and ask the students to walk about the room in any direction. Whenever you clap your hands, they must change direction. Next ask them to make eye contact with someone and not to break it even if they change direction. Then ask them to shake hands and say hello to everyone they meet.

Next, give a high five to everyone they meet. Then tell everyone they meet one thing about themselves. Then tell everyone they meet the name of a vegetable, their favourite dinosaur, someone they'd like to be, their favourite dinner, that they love them …

Once again you can do whatever you like with this activity; as long as everyone is enjoying it and they keep moving, you can't fail.

This is a quick and easy game that can be utilised anytime you want to inject a bit of energy into the proceedings.

85 Should've Gone to Specsavers

Time: *5 mins*

Additional Resources: *none*

Students get to have their eyes tested

When the students are seated and comfortable explain that you have changed five things about the classroom. The students, in pairs, then have three minutes to guess what you've changed.

Despite the fact that the students spend time in this room, when did they last really look at it and take in what is going on around them? We all look but do we really see? To be fully open and focused requires us all to look at things in a different way as if through a new set of eyes.

You may be surprised by what you see or miss on a regular basis. To prove this point, go onto YouTube and search for 'awareness test moonwalking bear'.

86

Chinese Whispers

Time: *5 mins*

Additional Resources: *none*

A student summarises what they've learned in the lesson and passes it down the line. Will it be the same at the end of the line?

This simple version of Chinese whispers allows the main message of a lesson to be repeated by all students in a fun and quick activity. Make sure the person you choose to start the whisper is likely to offer a good answer!

This could also be used at the start of a lesson if you want to recap on the learning from last time.

87

Jingle Bell

Time: *5 mins*

Additional Resources: *none*

Students create a rhyme to save time

Five minutes before the end of the session ask the students to shout out an even number between one and ten, say four for instance. The students must then construct a four-line jingle that reviews the key message of the lesson before the bell goes. Those that complete a jingle get to say it and then go. Those that don't produce one must wait till everyone else has gone. Ha ha!

The students might like to record these jingles on their phones as a future learning resource.

88

A Sweet Focus

Time: *5–10 mins*

Additional Resources: *a bag of sweets*

Students are invited to focus on an object and experience it fully

Hand around one wrapped sweet for each student. Introduce this as a lesson in focus. Ask everyone to place the sweet in front of them and look at it. Encourage them to look carefully and notice more. See the colour, shape and so on. Move on to handling the sweet and noticing its weight, texture and firmness. What emotions are they going through as they visualise eating the sweet? Can they imagine what it will taste like? When they eat the sweet, encourage a full experience of the flavours released in different parts of the mouth.

If you're a bit of a hippy at heart like me, you could even take the group outside to focus on a tree.

89 Sweet Russian Roulette

Time: *5 mins*

Additional Resources: *bag of sweets*

Students play a version of Russian roulette but with a sweet rather than a bullet

This is a good follow-up to the previous activity. Reveal to students that you are going to give out one sweet to each person, but that one of the sweets is a trick sweet (the sort you get from a joke shop) and will taste disgusting. The rest of the sweets are normal. Give out the sweets then ask students to look at theirs and describe their feelings to their partner or table. Allow the students to eat their sweet.

Obviously, you don't actually need to include a nasty sweet. Just calling one 'the vomit sweet' tends to grab the attention of a group sufficiently.

Emotions such as excitement, nervousness, relief and disappointment are usually experienced. Much of life follows a similar pattern.

90

All Tied Up

Time: *5 mins*

Additional Resources: *at least 1 school tie*

Students get to solve a problem that will tie them up in knots

Set the students the following task: holding a school tie at both ends, and without letting go, is it possible to get a knot tied in the middle?

The trick is to start with your arms folded (properly) and then grab on to each end of the tie. As you unfold your arms a knot will appear.

This is a terrific way to see how creative the students are at problem solving and whether they have the capacity to think divergently as well as logically.

91

Exit Pass

Time: 5 mins

Additional Resources: none

Students are encouraged to summarise their learning before they are allowed to leave the room

At the start of the lesson announce that students are only allowed to exit at the end of the session if they can share something they have learned or enjoyed during the lesson. This technique encourages students to focus but be vigilant as it may also prompt them to climb out of windows.

This activity works best in the class prior to lunch or home time, and is best undertaken at the end of a session.

92 Whose School is it Anyway?

Time: *10–15 mins*

Additional Resources: *paper and pens*

The group explores what they really think about their school (or other grouping)

Is your class/school focused on a common goal or purpose? In this activity you may discover the answer.

Hand each student a sheet of A4 and ask them to write a one-sentence answer to the following question:

What is our school/class purpose?

Students could be invited to share their responses in groups before feeding back to the whole group. Is there consistency within the answers? What purpose would your students prefer? A new school motto could be on the way.

This is an adaptation of a game used in business settings as described by Daniel Pink in his book Drive. A variation of the game is to ask students to draw an answer to the question:

If this school were an animal or mode of transport, what would it be?

Encourage students to explore their metaphor with questions such as: What is the food/power source? Where do the students and staff fit in?

93 Better Ways to Focus?

Time: *5–10 mins*

Additional Resources: *copy sheet (overleaf) for each student*

Students are asked to guess which goal-planning techniques are best

Here are two lists outlining ways to focus on an important goal or ambition:

List 1

- Make a plan broken into steps

- Share your goals with people you admire/respect

- Think about how good you'll feel when you achieve your goal

- Record and reward yourself for making progress

List 2

- Think about someone you admire who has achieved the same goal you are attempting

- Keep your goal to yourself

- Think about how bad you'll feel if you don't achieve your goal

- Think about how much other people will admire you if you achieve your goal

Ask students to consider both lists and agree which, if either, is more likely to be successful. They may use examples of goals their parents or friends have attempted, such as weight loss or changing job. They may explore goals they have attained or failed to stick to, such as hobbies, sports or learning to play the bagpipes.

List 1

1. Make a plan broken into steps

   ....

   ....

   ....

   ....

2. Share your goals with people you admire/respect

3. Think about how good you'll feel when you achieve your goal

4. Record and reward yourself for making progress

   ....

   ....

   ....

   ....

List 2

1. Think about someone you admire who has achieved the same goal you are attempting

2. Keep your goal to yourself

3. Think about how bad you'll feel if you don't achieve your goal

4. Think about how much other people will admire you if you achieve your goal

You can download printable versions of these sheets from our website here:
www.needsfocusedteaching.com/changemood-resources

Research by Richard Wiseman, described in his book 59 Seconds, concludes that people who use the methods outlined in List 1 are far more likely to achieve their goals; List 2 activities seem to make people more likely to fail.

94

Pull My Finger

Time: *5 mins*

Additional Resources: *none*

Don't panic – it's not what you think!

Ask the students to stand in a circle with their left hand sticking out, palm up to their left side. Their right hand should be held out to the right-hand side in a fist with the index finger pointing down, touching the middle of the left palm of the person next to them. The object of the activity (on the count of 3) is to grab the finger of the person on their left whilst evading the capture of their right index finger by the person on their right.

It sounds complicated, but it isn't. What it is though is hilarious, as the group usually breaks out in hysterics – as the tension mounts and resolve is broken (but not, hopefully, fingers).

A superb energiser that can be used at a moment's notice, in order to get the students simultaneously buzzing and focused.

95

Recipe for Success

Time: *10 mins*

Additional Resources: *none*

Students are invited to share their favourite recipe for a successful future

You may wish to put your own spin on this activity, but for convenience I'll provide you with an easy-to-use template. The students may want to name the dish after the job title they are after. For example, we will be making an actor, accompanied with educationalist and writer, and a side order of presenter served on a bed of stand-up comedian.

Ingredients

Bravery - 2 very large spoonfuls

Energy - 1 whole packet

Creativity - hundreds and thousands

Openness - ready-rolled

Motivation - pre-prepared

Confidence - as much as you can find

Method

Blend ingredients together, put into a warm and friendly environment and allow to simmer for ten years. Eventually bring to the boil and serve when ready, making sure there is enough to go round and that everyone gets a taste.

Best served with family, friends and a captive audience.

Warning! May contain nuts.

The students can keep this recipe as a gentle reminder for when things get tough. You may like to create a recipe book filled with all these tasty futures.

96

Mind Reader

Time: *5 mins*

Additional Resources: *3 (nearly) identical cups or containers*

The teacher creates the impression that they can read the minds of their students – a guaranteed way to get a group to focus

Many great magicians have delighted and amazed audiences with illusions built around the following basic idea.

Three cups or other containers are placed on a table. You invite a student to hide a personal object beneath one of the containers while you are not looking. Ask them to complicate matters by swapping the positions of the two empty cups. You then look at the cups and predict accurately which cup hides their object.

The effect is made possible by ensuring one of the containers is marked in a subtle way. To guess which cup contains the object you simply look for the marked container. If it is in the same position, it must contain the object. If the marked container has moved the hidden object must be in the one position the marked container hasn't appeared in (i.e. the before or after position). Practise this a couple of times and it becomes obvious. You can achieve the same effect with playing cards.

You need to big up your acting skills to maximise the impact. Strain and concentrate as you make a big show of 'reading the mind' of your volunteer. Perhaps claim you are great at reading body language and can tell when someone is lying. (This could be useful later in the year if students believe you can read their minds. If you think this is unethical just don't play for money, especially if you work in a primary school. That was a joke; by all means fleece them!)

97 Focus On Me, Please

Time: *10 mins*

Additional Resources: *none*

Students experience, vote on and practise ways to positively influence others just by the way they speak

The brain has an amazing capacity to conceive and create music, art and inventions when it is focused on a task. It's true that it also solves problems by accident as well as design, but it is at the moment of focusing that the magic is applied and brought to life. Practising how to encourage others to focus on us and listen to what we have to say is important in life. There are times when we would like to be seen and heard.

This experiment will help students explore three ways to boost their communication skills. Ask students to vote on which approach creates more focus.

Stand still or moving?

Give out an instruction first while moving around and handing out paper. Follow up with an instruction while standing and making eye contact with some of the students. The vote should reveal the second approach is more effective. An example of this at home would be the difference between a parent shouting up the stairs for their child to turn down the hip-hop, and going upstairs to talk face-to-face about the acceptable level.

Deep or high pitch voice?

We all have a range within our voice. Let's say our normal voice is 10 on a scale from 1 to 20. Ask the group to count out loud from 10 up to their highest, squeakiest voice at 20. Then go back down from 10 to 1, with 1 being their deepest voice, like a voice-over to a horror movie. Give out an instruction with your voice at level 8, then follow it with an instruction at level 12. Take a vote on the most effective. The deeper voice tends to carry far greater authority. The group can practise asking each other to do things with different voices. As an example, ask the group if they know when their parents mean business just through the level of their voice (they do).

Aussie rules or not?

A downward inflection at the end of a sentence adds gravity as it is a command, whereas an upward inflection lacks gravity as it is a question (except in Australia or the US where there is a tendency to finish every sentence with an upward inflection). Students could practise with the statement, 'I'd really like to borrow your pencil, Sheila, as mine is broken.' Antipodean accent optional.

These techniques are great for teachers and students as they provide us with the skills to be listened to without resorting to shouting, anger or force.

98 Playing with Perception

Time: *5-10 mins*

Additional Resources: *3 containers for hottish, warm and cold water. They need to be large enough for a volunteer to immerse their hands*

Students experience a trick of perception which messes with reality

Three watertight containers large enough to accommodate a hand submerged in water are each half-filled with water of differing temperatures. One-litre ice cream tubs are ideal. So, this game provides the ideal excuse to gorge on ice cream – you're doing it for the kids!

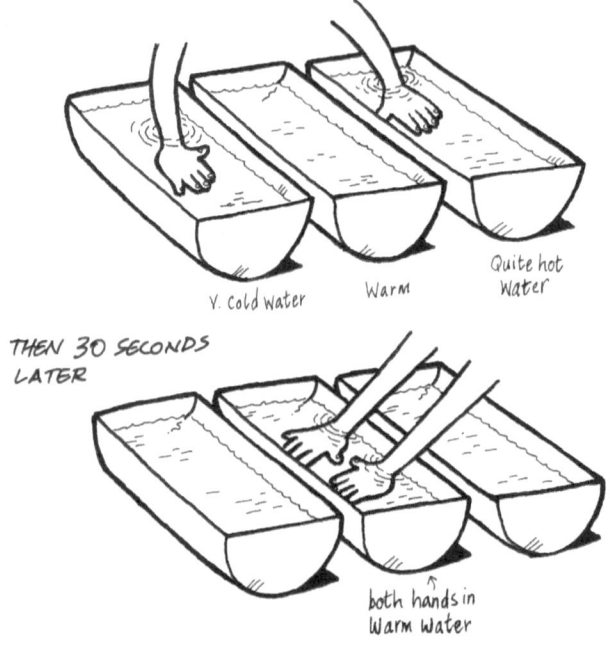

V. Cold Water   Warm   Quite hot Water

THEN 30 SECONDS LATER

both hands in Warm Water

Into one container pour very cold water (add a few ice cubes if possible), in the next lukewarm water, and in the third, warm-to-hot water. Volunteers are asked to put one hand in the cold water and the other in the hottish water for around thirty seconds (it's longer than you think). They then put both hands in the lukewarm water. They will experience a different feeling of heat in each hand even though the water surrounding both hands is the same.

This activity gives students the opportunity to focus intently on physical sensations and is a great metaphor for learning and perception vs reality.

99

Disappearing Paper

Time: *5 mins*

Additional Resources: *toilet tissue (A4 paper is an acceptable substitute)*

The teacher makes something disappear (and no, it doesn't work with a class you'd rather not teach)

Another trick we can share that is unlikely to have the Magic Circle calling their lawyers is the disappearing toilet paper. This happens in many school toilets without the use of magic. The teacher should ask the audience not to spoil the trick but just work out if they can see how it is done on their own.

The teacher scrunches a piece of toilet paper (or tissue or other light paper). They place it in their clenched hand and ask a volunteer to blow on it three times to make it disappear. Between each blow the teacher, in very theatrical sweeps, moves their arms around the head of the student and asks them to concentrate hard on making the object vanish, and to keep very still. After the third blow the hand is opened and the object has indeed vanished.

The trick is to throw away the object behind the head of the volunteer after the second blow (when the hand is above eye level). Simple but fun. You can add to the impact of this trick by asking for a second student to stand behind the volunteer. Let them know beforehand they are going to catch the object and place it in their pocket or – for a truly impressive finale – the jacket pocket of the volunteer!

Things that seem baffling and confusing can be understood once we know how they are done. A different perspective or viewpoint results in different experiences.

100

Complimentary Gift

Time: *5 mins*

Additional Resources: *none*

Students are encouraged to leave the teacher a parting gift

My daughters attend a school where at the end of the day the students shake hands with the teacher and thank them. I like this simple, yet respectful and significant, interaction between student and teacher.

This activity takes it one stage further and asks that the students not only shake hands and say, 'thank you', but also give one reason why they enjoyed the lesson.

This is both a quick review for the student and a positive confidence booster for the teacher. We need them too!

101 How Long Will I Live For?

Time: 5 mins

Additional Resources: none

A good question and a game that can be played using statistics and a metaphorical pinch of salt

Students are asked to write down a series of numbers based on their answers to the following questions. They use the numbers to predict their lifespan.

Ask students to make a note of the numbers as you read through the following questions:

Will you get married? (Yes +8, No or not sure 0)

Do you enjoy regular activity? (Yes +2, No 0)

Are you are a couch potato? (Yes -8)

Are you tidy? (Yes +1)

Are you an only child? (Yes -5)

Are you female? (Yes +10)

Are you male and shorter than 1.8m (5' 9')? (Yes +5)

Do you eat mostly fast-food? (Yes -4)

Do you smoke? (Yes -8)

Do you have a pet? (Yes +2)

Do you laugh regularly? (Yes +1)

Are you going to have a good work–life balance? (Yes +3)

Add 70 to the points gained or lost above and you will have an estimate of your likely lifespan (subject to accidents, advances in medical science and earth being smashed to bits by an asteroid.

The above factors can start a good discussion and for most of them we have a real choice which can influence our lifespan. These statistics should be taken with a pinch of salt – we want to enlighten not frighten our students. It is also worth remembering that life is not just about how long we live for; it is also about what we're living for. It's about putting more life in our days, not just more days in our life.

For more statistics see The Long Life Equation by Trisha Macnair.

102 The Most Valuable Resource

Time: 10 mins

Additional Resources: balloon, hairy head and empty aluminium can

Following an optional demonstration, students are challenged to agree upon or justify the most precious invisible resource

Explain to your group that you are going to demonstrate the power of invisible forces. Blow up a balloon and rub it against a hairy head to create static, but beware unicorn hair clips. Place the balloon near to an empty can lying on its side, as illustrated below. Observe the can being pulled toward the balloon.

Challenge students to identify the invisible. There are many invisible forces, things and beliefs: gravity, religion, love, time, hope, consciousness, electricity, oxygen and so on.

John Lloyd, speaking on www.ted.com, eloquently argues that all the most important things in life are things we cannot see. We often ignore or dismiss the invisible. This is dangerous, as many are the most important things in the world.

Did you like these activities?
Would you like more?

Get your FREE pack of fun classroom games, activities, fill-ins and more right here:

www.needsfocusedteaching.com/changemood-resources

Download your pack for free right now...

References

Claxton, Guy (2008). *What's the Point of School? Rediscovering the Heart of Education.* Oxford: Oneworld.

Csikszentmihalyi, Mihaly (2002). *Flow: The Psychology of Happiness.* London: Random House.

Engleman, Marge (2001). *Aerobics of the Mind Cards: 100 Exercises for a Healthy Brain.* Verona, WI: Attainment Company.

Gardner, Howard (1993). *Frames of Mind.* London: Fontana.

Gilbert, Ian (2011) *Why do I Need a Teacher When I've Got Google?* London: Routledge/Farmer.

Glenn, Jim and Denton, Carey (2003). *Encyclopedia of Family Games.* London: Reader's Digest.

Holden, Robert (2008). *Success Intelligence: Essential Lessons and Practices from the World's Leading Coaching Program on Authentic Success.* New York: Hay House.

MacDonald, Glynn (1994). *The Alexander Technique (Headway Lifeguides).* London: Hodder Arnold.

Macnair, Trisha (2007). *The Long Life Equation: 100 Factors That Can Add or Subtract Years from Your Life.* London: New Holland.

Mosley, Jenny and Sonnet, Helen (2003). *101 Games for Social Skills.* Hyde: LDA.

Neill, Michael (2009). *Supercoach: 10 Secrets to Transform Anyone's Life.* London: Hay House.

Pink, Daniel H. (2009). *Drive: The Surprising Truth about What Motivates Us.* New York: Riverhead Books.

Reeves, Richard (2003). *The Politics of Happiness.* London: New Economics Foundation.

Stewart, Trenton Lee (2007). *The Mysterious Benedict Society.* New York: Little, Brown and Company.

Wenger, Win and Poe, Richard (2000). *The Einstein Factor*. Niles, IL: Nightingale-Conant.

Wilkinson, Richard and Pickett, Kate (2010). *The Spirit Level*. London: Penguin.

Wiseman, Richard (2009). *59 Seconds: Think a Little, Change a Lot*. London: Macmillan.

Zenon, Paul (2003). *100 Ways to Win a Tenner*. London: Carlton Books.

Index

 Energy

Calm

Creative Thinking

 Connection

 Focus

Made in United States
Troutdale, OR
05/25/2024

20101255R00096